When Jerusalem Burned

When Jerusalem Burned

Gérard Israel
and
Jacques Lebar

Translated from the French
by Alan Kendall

William Morrow & Company, Inc.
NEW YORK   1973

Acknowledgements

Grateful acknowledgement is made to Penguin Books Ltd. for permission to reprint extracts from *The Dead Sea Scrolls* and *The Jewish War*; and for the use of the following illustrations: Bust of Titus and Triumph of Titus, to Giraudon; Model of Jerusalem, to Israel Colour Slides Ltd. Jerusalem.

The authors wish to thank George Weill, paleographic archivist and head of the library service of the Alliance Israélite Universelle, Rabbi E. Gourevitch, head of the Hebraica Section and Jacques Peuchmaurd and Max Gallo, for their most helpful advice.

Printed in the United States of America.

Library of Congress Catalog Card Number 73-4228

Contents

136223

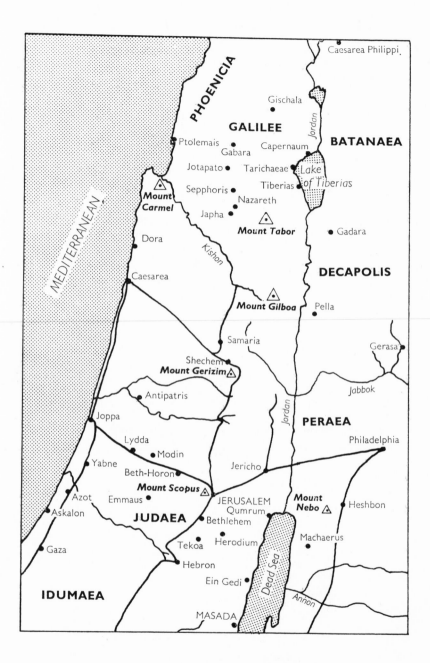

Chronology

BC

1650-1500	The patriarchs: Abraham, Isaac, Jacob. The birth of monotheism.
1500-1300	The Hebrews enslaved in Egypt.
1300	Moses leads the Hebrews out of Egypt.
1225-1020	The Judges, heroes of the nation, wield authority over the Jewish people.
1020-1004	Saul first King of Israel.
1004-965	David King of Israel.
965-926	Solomon builds the First Temple.
733-732	Assyrian invasions.
605	Battle of Carchemish.
598	Nebuchadnezzar, King of Babylon, invades Judaea.
586	Fall of Jerusalem and destruction of Solomon's Temple by Nebuchadnezzar. The Jews are deported to Babylon.
549-539	Cyrus the Great, King of the Persians, invades and conquers Babylon.
538	Cyrus authorizes the Jews in Babylon to return to Judaea and rebuild the Temple.
520-516	Zerubbabel builds the Second Temple.

500	Preaching of Malachi, the last prophet.
458	Ezra brings a second contingent of Jews to Judaea from Babylon.
445-433	Nehemiah rekindles the religious fervour of the Jews.
332	Alexander the Great enters Judaea.
200-198	Antiochus III, King of Syria, conquers Judaea.
175-168	Antiochus IV, Epiphanes, persecutes the Jews and desecrates the Temple.
167	Beginning of the Maccabean revolt.
165	Rededication of the Temple.
160	Death of Judas Maccabaeus.
143	Death of Jonathan Maccabaeus.
140	Death of Simeon Maccabaeus, Prince of Israel.
134	Rome recognizes the independence of Judaea.
134-104	John Hyrcanus King and High Priest of Israel.
104-76	Alexander Jannaeus King and High Priest of Israel.
76-67	Reign of Alexandra Salome.
66-63	Aristobulus II and Hyrcanus II struggle for power in Judaea.
63	Pompey conquers Judaea and desecrates the Holy of Holies.
48-44	Caesar master of Rome.
39	Herod King of Judaea.
27-14 (AD)	Augustus first Emperor of Rome.
9	Herod extends and beautifies the Temple.

4   Death of Herod and birth of Jesus of Nazareth.
     Rule of Roman procurators and formation of Zealot party.

AD

14   Death of Augustus and Accession of Tiberius.

37-41   Caligula Emperor of Rome.

41-54   Claudius Emperor of Rome.

54   Accession of Nero.

66   Judaeo-Roman war.

69   Vespasian Emperor of Rome.

70   Roman legions burn and raze the Temple.
      Creation of the religious schools.

73   Fall of Masada

79   Titus Emperor of Rome.

98   Trajan Emperor of Rome.

112   Revolt of the Jews of the Diaspora.

117   Hadrian Emperor of Rome

132   Bar Kochba revolt and fall of Bethar.

135   Hadrian decides to build a pagan altar on the Temple site.

323   Emperor Constantine is converted to Christianity.

Preface

The story you are about to read is of an event which concerns the Jewish people and all men adhering to monotheism, and which occurred nineteen hundred years ago, in the year 70 on the day which is, by the Hebrew calendar, the ninth day of the month of Ab (July-August).

On that day the Roman soldiers burned and destroyed the Temple at Jerusalem. On that day the Jewish soul was struck at its very core.

From the time of Moses until the capture of Jerusalem, Judaism had been built on the two pillars of national and religious tradition—each one firmly overlapping the other.

When Jewish nationality as such dissolved in the wake of the Roman victory, the religious element in Judaism took priority. The Temple at Jerusalem was the only place where ritual sacrifice might be made, but it had been destroyed. Nevertheless, the Jews of the Diaspora were determined to preserve their identity, and adapted themselves to the changed conditions. Since the one Temple had ceased to exist they created other fortresses in which to entrench themselves. These were the synagogues and places of study—all of which kept the flame burning in myriad Jewish communities.

Priests and aristocrats were succeeded by scholars and rabbis, the tireless dispensers of traditional teaching. Henceforth it was the study of the Law which prevailed, and which preserved the supranational links among Jews who were scattered throughout Christian or Islamic societies.

It was almost nineteen hundred years before the wounds began to heal, wounds inflicted on the descendants of the defenders of the Temple, who lived among other nations and experienced the terrible sufferings that occurred in the Diaspora. Then, in 1948, with the resurrection of a Jewish state, a new fusion of nationhood and religion suddenly became possible. Was the creation of the new state an extraordinary and rather late revenge on the Roman Empire, whose power and whose gods had now disappeared for ever? Had the nineteen hundred years since 70 been only a very long period in the wilderness, an agonized interlude in Jewish continuity?

The history of the West is also tied to the event of the 9th of Ab, 70.

In the destruction of the Temple, which Jesus had frequented, the first Christians saw the proof of the arrival of a new world. The Gentiles, who worshipped stone gods, considered the Jews' endless struggle against Roman might—in the name of a unique and invisible God and following on the violation of the Temple—an amazing act of courage which never ceased to astonish them. Some actually became Jews; others—more numerous—became Christians. The Roman Empire collapsed. How did these things happen? Why was the Temple destroyed?

Unlike other great events in Antiquity, and even in times nearer to our own, all the consequences of the battle and fall of Jerusalem have not yet run their course.

Prologue A Heap of Ruins

A flaming torch thrown by a Roman soldier was to change the destiny of of a nation.

For almost one hundred days he had been there, one among the 15,000 of Titus' men who were besieging the Temple of the Jews at Jerusalem. Possibly this soldier was not a Roman. He might have been Egyptian or Syrian, Greek or Gaul; history does not say. In the vast Roman war machine, nothing distinguished him from his comrades in arms: no item of clothing or belief. In common with all Roman soldiers he wore the reddish cloak, the helmet with its mane, the breast-plate feared throughout the world. In common with all Roman soldiers, he fought to establish imperial peace.

That day a furious attack by the beleaguered Jews had brought him into the front line of battle; but once again the order and discipline of the cohorts had defeated the uncontrolled efforts of the worshippers of the invisible God. No one remembered the soldier's name, and the role that he played was no more important that that of the other men. He had done what he had been trained to do like clockwork: fight organized war, mechanized war, war in the Roman way. But after the final effort which ended the sally of the besieged, that soldier had found himself almost alone at the base of the Temple wall, and for the first time, like someone in a state of stupefaction, he had acted in an anarchistic manner: without calculation, without discipline, without a command. The Roman soldier had noticed that one of the Temple windows was close at hand, apparently unguarded—and decided to light a piece of wood It was an easy thing to do, since August of the year AD 70 was a torrid month, and the wood burned quickly. Then, getting another soldier to help him, he had hauled himself up on to a comrade's shoulders, clung to the wall, and thrown the burning brand inside the building which no Gentile had ever desecrated without causing a catastrophe.

The burning of the Temple of Jerusalem began, and nothing could stop it—not the cries of the priests nor the efforts of the Jewish fighters, nor the wrath of Titus who, a few days previously, in the course of a dramatic council meeting, had decided that he would not destroy the holy place after the Jews' inevitable capitulation. Paradoxically, both Roman and Jew tried to avert the disaster, but their efforts were in vain.

The Roman soldier had set off a chain reaction of events the consequences of which, nineteen centuries later, are still not spent. Slowly he moved away from the wall and turned towards Jerusalem, spread out at his feet and already defeated. He knew the Jewish holy city well. On several occasions it had fallen to his lot to leave the garrison in Caesarea and come within the shadow of this city to keep order when Jews from far and wide arrived on pilgrimage to sacrifice to their God in His Temple. He had himself—the very epitome of order—mounted guard on the Temple gates, and forbidden Gentiles to cross the limits that the religion of Israel fixed for them. He had patrolled Jerusalem so that Roman order would be respected, had taken his turn as a sentry at the Antonia fortress which dominated the Temple, from where the business of watching the Jews was child's play. In spite of its mysteries, Jerusalem held no secrets for him. When he arrived there for the first time from the north, on the road from Caesarea, he had found a city resembling a lion skin thrown over a chair—a city possessing a dirty yellow hue, that was built on hills which gave the impression of unrest and torment. But it was from Mount Scopus, some 2,500 feet high, that the holy city of the Jews appeared in all its splendour, with the sanctuary of Israel at its centre. The several hills, crossed by the deep valleys of Kedron, Gehenna and the Tyropoeon, enfolded the upper city and the scattered, spacious dwellings of the rich, while in the lower town were concentrated the vast majority of the 100,000 inhabitants. The constant sentry on Mount Scopus, who continually watched the only natural means of access to Jerusalem, the one from the north, could—by turning his back on the city—see in fine weather the Dead Sea which, like a sheet of metal, reflected the straight beams of the sun back at the sky, as if to magnify their intensity. Under the effects of this supernatural light, the mountains of Judaea lost all reality, all relief, all life. The light in Jerusalem had a soul, it gave objects and people a new and renewed dimension. it vibrated in the open sky and plunged into the shadow of the city as if to combat the forces of evil there. On occasions, as on that day for example, the burning wind of Asia—the Khamsin—came into the very heart of the town. Then nothing moved, neither beast nor man, as all creatures awaited the liberating breath of wind from the sea, which came leaping over the mountains and plunging down

* *

into the town again like a furious wave imprisoned by a jagged, rocky coast.

The Roman soldier was no stranger to the town and its people. He had mingled with the crowd, particularly with the unemployed who, since the completion of the Temple, had taken to the alleys of the city, looking for some little job or other and falling prey to the revolutionary sentiments expressed by nameless leaders. In that city everyone seemed to know everyone else. Life there was provincial, and had nothing in common with the life Roman citizens were able to lead in Rome or Alexandria—each cities of a million inhabitants. The streets were narrow. It was impossible for carts to move through them and difficult for the Roman cavalry to get about. Heavily laden donkeys could scarcely pass, and caused inextricable traffic jams. The flocks of animals driven to the Temple for sacrifice bumped into everything in their path. The water carrier, with his water-skin on his shoulder, was hardly able to find enough space to pour the precious liquid into a copper goblet without spilling it on the ground.

Every district of Jerusalem—though this fact did not surprise the Roman soldier—had its own profession. The carpenters, the dyers, the money-changers and the smiths were together, but it was the same in all the towns of the inhabited world. Jerusalem, however, had no gardens, no open spaces. Everything was taken up by the life of men. The Jews, always busy, always on the move, had no statues to pause before, no monuments to detract from the cult of the one God who dwelt only in the Temple.

The smells of Jerusalem, also, were strange to the Roman. When the wind was in the north-east the emanations of burning fat from the sacrificed animals invaded the city and clung to its inhabitants' clothing. And then, of course, there were the Jews themselves, with their deep black curly hair. The young rarely cut their hair, so that they all appeared to have manes of jet. The old people cut their hair more often, but the bald —of whom there were few—were frequently the object of derision, since hair was widely held to be a sign of strength.

The Jews of Judaea had a national costume. Only the colour and the amount of wear distinguished the rich from the poor. The clothing of the rich was red, purple or crimson, and sometimes embroidered. That of the poor was grey or brown. But everyone wore a linen coat with sleeves and a full, long shirt, tied with a belt—and over this a kind of shawl with a blue thread at the four corners, to which the Jews attached a religious significance. Possibly they intended to distinguish themselves from the Gentiles in this way, though the soldier had noticed the different clothing worn by the Jews who lived outside Judaea and who came on pilgrimages to the Temple.

The Jews from Babylon could be picked out by their long black robes which trailed on the ground; those from Phoenicia by their long, multi-coloured trousers; those from Anatolia by their goat hair surcoats; and those from Persia by their magnificent silk clothing embroidered in silver or gold.

All these people were in a perpetual state of movement. Even the women, often discreetly veiled, passed by quickly and busily. The intrepid nature of the calvary patrols, the pride of the Roman army, gave the world of Jerusalem a sharp note of contrast.

But that day Jerusalem was deserted. All had been killed or were in flight, and when the Roman cohorts went up to strengthen the force around the Temple, they did not encounter the usual busy crowd of the city of the God of the Jews. Only a black or ochre pall of smoke rose from the city towards the Temple, as if to maintain a last bond of intimacy with Him whom the Temple still protected.

*   *   *

The soldier brushed away the comrade who had helped him to reach the golden window. Slowly he looked up towards the opening and heard the dry crackle of wood taking light. A cloud of smoke suddenly billowed up, and perhaps he realized that the last fire of the last temple of the Jews was beginning. But the rising smoke and the falling smoke, that of the city and that of the Temple, joined, blotting out the soldier who, without realizing it, had passed into history.

In a few hours the whole of the Temple was alight; in a few days there was not one stone left upon another. The Temple of the Jews passed into the memory of the Jews—but first, according to tradition, the young priests who survived gathered on the roof of the sanctuary. One of them shouted out: 'Master of the Universe, since You have not thought us worthy to be Your faithful servants, receive back these keys'—and he threw the keys into the sky. Then, as legend has it, a hand came out of Heaven and took them, as the priests threw themselves into the flames.

*   *   *

Seventy years later a man made his way towards the ruins of the Temple. Nothing had changed in the city since the Jewish resistance ended with the collective suicide of the defenders of Masada, the chief fortress of Israel. In Jerusalem, one Roman legion—the Tenth—remained to prevent Jewish vagabonds and ragamuffins from approaching the site of the sanctuary. For decades these Jews had wandered in and about the city like wild dogs, though they knew full well that nothing remained of the Temple Herod had built—the Temple which, more than anything else in their history, had kept the link between created and Creator. There was nothing—apart from a wall on the west which, seven decades earlier, Titus had planned to use as a support for the foundations of a new citdael.

For a whole year the Tenth Roman Legion had remained adamant: no one was allowed through. But on the ninth day of the month of Ab—a double anniversary of the destruction of Solomon's temple by Nebuchadnezzar and Herod's temple by Titus—the soldiers relented and the Jews hurried to the wall to weep there. Quickly they crossed the city, and as they passed a few half-wild animals ran out of their haunts in the gutted houses.

There was no trace of former Jewish existence. The two Roman camps showed their might on the northern side of the city, and their standards with the portraits of Roman emperors streamed in the wind. At the end of the day the Jews left the site of the former glory of Israel and for another year Jerusalem became again a powerfully guarded, closed city, left to its shadows.

He is there, many miles from Jerusalem, contemplating the course of events since he had dared defy the Emperor Hadrian. By forbidding circumcision throughout the Empire, by refusing to keep the promise he had once made to allow the Jews to rebuild their Temple, Hadrian had pushed him to the point of revolt. The man encamped at the gates of the ruined city and raised an immense army throughout the Diaspora—an army which in no way resembled a band of peasants in revolt. All his men were seasoned and trained. All had only four fingers on their left hand, for before enrolling them their leader had asked them to prove their courage by mutilating themselves. This, however, became too easy a proof, and was soon superseded by one imposed on all cavalry, namely of being able to uproot a Lebanon cedar at full tilt.

The man who had ruled the destiny of this army was greatly revered. People said that he was the Messiah, the man who was to rebuild the

Temple. He was called Bar Kochba, the son of the star, for had not the Torah said that a star would come forth out of Jacob? This man was gifted with incredible strength. It was said that he had repelled missiles with his foot, hurling them back and killing the men who fired the enemy catapults. Soldiers such as his had easily occupied Jerusalem and succesfully harried the retreating Romans. But such success did not necessarily mean that the objective of the mission had been accomplished, and when night fell over the dead city Bar Kochba realized he could not stop the next Roman assaults on a heap of ruins. He had no wall, no citadel, and no defensive position what was more, there was also the road from the north, which was wide open. Simon bar Giora's men, who held out against Titus for one hundred days, had been forced to build three walls to protect three lines of defence. So, although it was tempting to remain in Jerusalem and await divine intervention, Bar Kochba had ordered the retreat, thus creating the extraordinary spectacle of a victorious Jewish army voluntarily leaving the city where God dwelt.

The town of Bettar or Beth-ther, some six miles from Jerusalem, was a positive eagle's aery. In the immediate surroundings Bar Kochba had built fifty fortified places. There, for two-and-a-half years, the men of the son of the star resisted Hadrian's legions under the command of Severus. The Roman army, numbering some seventy thousand men, finally won; once again a Messiah was abandoned to die like any other, though with his weapons in his hands. On this occasion, 580,000 Jews were killed. The Talmud says: 'So many Jews were slaughtered that the horses were in blood up to their nostrils and the blood picked up pieces of rock weighing forty *seah* and carried them down to the sea, which it coloured with its red colour, four miles out from the bank. If it be thought that Bettar was close to the sea, it is an error: the town was forty miles away from it.'

After Bar Kochba's defeat, on the ninth day of the month of Ab in the year 135 of our era, the Jewish nation no longer existed. The man who fled from the scene of the slaughter in the middle of the night had only one desire, to leave Judaea where for thousands of years the Jews, whether free or under occupation, had undergone a thousand tortures and death in the name of the worship of their God and the concept of liberty they had made for themselves. He wanted to run to the limits of the inhabited world, to renounce everything, but above all to live. He was not a coward. He had fought, and his father and ancestors before him had fought, but they had all lost. He crossed the mountains of Judaea, the

Idumaean desert, avoided the burning summit of Mount Sinai (where the Law was given to his people), skirted the fertile valley of the Nile, crossed the deserts of Cyrene, followed the coast of Numidia, and went northwards towards the heart of Brittany. There he was consoled by the news that Hadrian had built on the site of the Temple of Jerusalem *Aelia Capitolina*, a sanctuary to Jupiter, in the middle of which stood an equestrian statue of the emperor. On his way he avoided the apprentice martyr Christians still talking about the saving Messiah, the redeeming God, and universal love and peace. He thus crossed the centuries and was only reconciled to himself on a plateau of Upper Silesia, in a little town called Auschwitz.

*   *   *

Another man did not choose war. Some time before Titus destroyed the Temple, he decided to leave Jerusalem. He was a Pharisee and a scholar of the Law. One may picture him in the Jewish national costume. He was certainly very old and looked fragile. He had a white beard and long smooth hair. The skin of his face was almost transparent, illuminated by deep eyes. This scholarly man knew that the temple would be destroyed and that the Jewish people would be dispersed. He wanted to save what he could. To do that he had to leave Jerusalem. In the middle of the night he woke three of his followers. They carried him out of Jerusalem as if he were dead. One took his head, the other his feet, and the third went in front. Covered with the traditional shroud embroidered at the corners with blue thread, one of the great masters of Judaism, Rabbi Johanan ben Zakkai, fled the besieged city.

It was pitch black when the three men and the rabbi reached the Roman lines. Sentries sprang out of the shadows and surrounded the Jews. One of them drew his sword to make sure that the corpse really was a corpse. One of Rabbi Johanan ben Zakkai's disciples stopped him and said: 'Do you want people to say, "One of their scholars is dead, killed by a Roman sword"?' They were allowed through. Rabbi Johanan was finally left in a cemetery. Despite the dark, the noise of the camp close by reached him. Slowly he went towards the spot in the camp where the Roman eagles could be heard flapping in the wind. He wandered for a while and then asked to see the king. The centurions laughed, pointing out that there was no king in that camp. Rabbi Johanan was eventually brought into the presence of Vespasian, the general in command of the Roman troops in Judaea. As soon as he saw the Roman general, Rabbi Johanan shouted '*Vive, domine imperator*'. Vespasian replied: 'You greet me as if I were the emperor, but I am not. If the emperor heard you, he would have me put to death.' Rabbi Johanan answered: 'If you are not ruler yet, you will be one day, because it is written that the Temple will only be destroyed by the hand of a king.' Vespasian was a man of modest origin, he had risen from the ranks and had never looked for honours. But these words did not surprise him. Already, during the taking of Jotapata, a Jewish governor called Josephus had made the same prediction. But this corroboration in the prophecy of the Jews inclined Vespasian towards generosity. The disciples of the old rabbi were allowed to leave beleaguered Jerusalem and follow their master, and Vespasian also granted Rabbi Johanan's request to open a school.

The rabbi and his disciples settled at Yabne (Jabneh or Jamnia), a little township on the coastal strip, situated on the same latitude as Jerusalem. Winter was gentle there, and summer oppressive. This town, or rather village, was on the great line of communication between Egypt and Syria.

When, on the ninth day of the month of Ab, the first refugees from Jerusalem arrived in Yabne and told of the destruction of the Temple, Rabbi Johanan tore his clothing, and his disciples did the same. They sobbed and wept and put on mourning. But the next day they were back at their studies. To ensure the survival of the people, Judaism must be kept alive, even without national independence, even without the Temple which was the House of God. The Jewish faith must become spiritual, and dissociate itself from one particular site. Without realizing the fact, Rabbi Johanan and his disciples had drawn up the classic model of the faiths we know, and thus the Jews, wherever they found themselves, wherever they were exiled, were able to re-establish the intimate link which bound them to the Almighty. This is what gave birth to prayer as it is said today, and which is in reality a substitute for the sacrifices carried out in the Temple. The first disciples of Jesus of Nazareth made a similar move, but in the eyes of the successors of Rabbi Johanan they went too far— much too far—in their task of replacing the worship of the Temple. For the School of Yabne also considered it important to uphold the religious values attached to the Jewish people itself. Prayer must remain collective, even if Israel was dispersed.

Rabbi Johanan ben Zakkai thought that Israel would be deprived of its Temple for a long time. This man—this mild and gentle man—vehemently opposed those of his disciples who wanted to turn Yabne into a new Jerusalem. One morning, to show that the religion of Moses had become universal in the heart of every Jew, he left Yabne and settled some way off. He knew, and he taught at the eventide of his life, that only a prophet announcing the arrival of the Messiah would be able to rebuild the Temple, in the newly found independence of the Jewish people.

Part One

THE GREAT CHALLENGE

1 The Jewish People, God and His Temple

'He is so seductive,' a courtesan used to say, 'that I can never leave him unless I give him a little bite.' Pompey was a happy man. At the age of twenty he had made a resounding entry into Roman Society. He was rich and came from an equestrian family. His vanity vied with his bravura and his military qualities. At the end of his African campaigns, he returned to Rome heady with success, determined to rule there. Sulla the dictator was anxious to handle this ambitious rival carefully, and so welcomed him at the city gates with the honours usually awarded to generals with long service behind them. But far from being satisfied with the title of *imperator*, Pompey demanded a triumph. Sulla refused, and the young wolf retorted, 'Let him take care, for the rising sun has more worshippers than the setting sun.' Sulla, with clenched fists, yielded: 'Let him triumph, let him triumph.'

Pompey was now forty. He had beaten Sertorius, a rebellious general, crushed the revolt of Spartacus, and in six weeks eliminated the pirates who were threatening to bring Rome to the point of starvation. But he continually dreamed of military exploits. An occasion arose. Mithridates, King of Pontus, was presenting a threat to Roman power by his activities in the area. Pompey was given supreme command. Fascinated by the Orient, he went to relieve Lucullus at the head of the Roman legions. The millionaire gourmet had already so weakened the enemy that operations degenerated into a military excursion. Mithridates fled towards the Caucasus. Deciding that pursuit was useless, the Roman general advanced towards Syria, where numerous tyrants had taken control of the various cities and the Arabs were plundering the countryside unchecked.

In 63 BC Judaea was geographically a part of Syria, but the Syrian and Jewish states were politically separate. Because of their length, the Syrian and Palestinian coasts destined these countries to be the scene of invasions and destructions, a meeting place for battles between preying powers. Because of its situation and its links with the Mediterranean, the Jewish state was therefore forced to make immense efforts towards its defence. The path of the Euphrates increased the danger even more. Rising in the Caucasus, the river flowed towards the Mediterranean, then turned sharply away. Between the river and Syria and Palestine were vast deserts. The predominant powers fought each other continuously to gain control of the upper reaches of the river which were close to fertile areas and the sea, and which enabled caravans and armies to avoid having to cross enormous desert stretches. When Egypt was powerful and her troops were bound for the North, they crossed Palestine, Phoenicia and Syria. Then when people from the East launched themselves into an attack on Egypt, they took the same route in the opposite direction. The coastal strip was nothing more than a corridor perpetually ravaged by destructive armies.

Pompey finished with turbulent Syria. When he reached Damascus he called his general staff together and had his officers explain the most recent developments in the fierce dynastic war then ravaging Judaea. Queen Salome's two sons were engaged in bloody fighting to win the throne. Hyrcanus II had been named as successor by his mother, but he was timid and weak, and was driven out of power by Aristobulus, a violent, unscrupulous man. The two brothers showered Pompey with gifts and flattery, and begged him to settle the dispute.

Pompey was scarcely conversant with the real situation in the kingdom and had no knowledge at all of the ancient Jewish traditions. Finding himself unceremoniously confronted with contradictory claims whose subtle theological and political content he barely understood, he prevaricated; but already he sensed the advantages to be gained by the Empire from the Judaean situation.

*   *   *

This was not the first time that Rome had intervened in Jewish affairs. Two hundred years earlier the Senate had managed to become friendly with Judaea when she was struggling against foreign domination.

Judaea was then subject to the pleasure of a Syrian monarch, Antiochus Epiphanes, who was obsessed with Hellenism. He was a clever politician, blinded with anti-Jewish hatred. Epiphanes means sent from God, but Jewish humorists nicknamed him Epimanes, which means mad.

The Jews had been the victims of an abject reign of terror and religious persecution, and yet they had also indulged in the worst sort of political and religious quarrels. The Hellenizing Jews, seduced by the refinements of Greek civilization, aped the manners of the occupying power. They decorated their homes with rare materials, and developed a taste for festivals with female dancers and singers. Their children packed the recently created gymnasia where the traditional Greek games took place, running, jumping, wrestling and boxing. The athletes were naked, and some young Jews lightly contravened the recommendations of holy scripture: 'Who so goeth naked in public places, there is no more vile and detestable person in the world.' Or elsewhere : 'Nakedness is dishonourable, it precedes stoning.' Some of them, to spare themselves the mockery of their playfellows when they went to bathe, underwent surgery in an attempt to conceal the marks of circumcision. Traitors worshipped pagan gods forcibly introduced by the tyrant. Doubt began to creep into people's minds—even the most sober: did traditional Jewish beliefs really correspond to the truth? Were not the Greeks right when they put pleasure before God? The Jewish aristocracy set an example of moral disintegration which easily took advantage of Antiochus Epiphanes' rule. Two conceptions of the world were in conflict. On the one hand there was the wisdom of the philosophers, the art of exact reasoning leading to knowledge, the freedom to choose one's gods and to worship them as one pleased; on the other, there was the worship of the one God, and fear in the face of the Eternal.

Antiochus, for his part, had thought only about the grand design of his reign, namely the destruction of Judaism and the suppression of Jewish laws and traditions. Step by step he had tentatively erected pagan altars in the countryside and small towns, and then—becoming bolder— he dared to install, with great pomp, a statue of Zeus in the Temple of Jerusalem—the Abomination of Desolation. Provocations had then followed each other in quick succession. The Sabbath and circumcision were forbidden, manuscripts of the Torah were consigned to bonfires, Jews were forced under torture to eat unclean meats. One of the king's men had even gone as far as to sacrifice pigs.

The village of Modin, near Jerusalem and not far from Lydda, had been the home of the Maccabees. In the market place a Jew was prostrate before a Greek statue and preparing to celebrate an act of religion. Mattathias, an old priest, was infuriated by this public sacrilege. He left the crowd and killed the traitor with a single sword stroke. Immediately his followers set upon a Syrian patrol, massacred the soldiers and knocked down both the altar and the statue. The spark of revolt had been struck. Mattathias and his sons—one of whom was called Judas —fled to the mountains and gave the word of command to the armed resistance. 'Do not fear the menaces of Antiochus, for all his glory is but dust, and one day he will be food for worms. He rises up today, but tomorrow he will disappear. Arm yourselves with courage and fight bravely for the defence of the Law, for it is that which will crown you with glory.'

The epic of fighting Judaea had begun. After underground activity, helped by the hilly terrain, and individual attacks on traitors, came pitched battles conducted by a great leader, Judas, who was known as Maccabaeus —the Hammer. When Antiochus saw his generals thoroughly beaten, he changed his tactics. Since the Jews had taken up arms, he would exterminate them. But Judas, at the head of a huge army, succeeded in isolating and entering Jerusalem—throwing the statues from the Temple and restoring traditional worship there.

Rome's rulers were happy to see Syrian power shaken by the struggle of the Jewish nationalists, and the Senate made discreet overtures to Judas, who responded by sending ambassadors to the capital of the Empire to negotiate the assistance of Rome against the excesses of the persecutors of his people. The talks ended in agreement.

Immediately the Jews published the text of the first Judaeo-Roman treaty:

'May all go well for the Romans and for the people of the Jews on land and on sea, for ever. May the sword and the enemy stay far from them. But should war threaten Rome first, or any single one of her allies at whatsoever point at which she is in control, the Jewish people, in response to the needs of the situation, will take part in the fight without reservation. And there will be given to the combatants no wheat, arms, money or ships, as Rome has decided it, but they will fulfil their obligations even though they receive nothing. Similarly, if war comes to the Jewish people, the Romans will take part in the fight with all their souls in response to the needs of the situation. And to the allies there will be given neither wheat, arms, money nor ships, as Rome has decided it, but they will fulfil these obligations, and that without fraud. This is what in these terms the Romans have agreed with the people of the Jews. Concerning the wrongs which King Demetrios has committed against the Jews, we have written to him: "Why have you made your burden heavy on our friends the Jews, our allies? If they complain again we will do justice to them, and will make war on you by land and by sea." '

The defeat and death in battle of Judas Maccabaeus in 160 did not end the Jewish struggle for freedom. The Maccabean War lasted for twenty-five years, led successively by Judas' two brothers, Simeon and

Jonathan, the High Priest. Slowly the Syrians were pushed back and the country recovered its complete independence. After four hundred years of Persian and Greek oppression, national liberation had finally come.

*   *   *

Pompey meditated for a long time. He knew now that he was going to invade Judaea. He scarcely worried about the mad struggle of the two brothers Hyrcanus and Aristobulus. The glory and tranquillity of Rome was of more importance than the intrigues of these kinglet candidates who vied for his protection. Was he then to force a conclusion? Why not? The Syrian Empire had ceased to exist. There was no interest whatsoever in an independent Judaea as far as Rome was concerned. A Jewish state, jealous of its liberties, would appear to Syria, which was now simply a Roman province, as an example and model. Pompey came down in favour of Hyrcanus, whose listlessness and servility he had detected at a glance.

The ousted Aristobulus made a show of resistance, but soon complied and even proposed handing over the Holy City. But his troops did not support him and, rejecting any idea of capitulation, they barricaded themselves behind the walls of the Temple.

While the siege was getting under way and Pompey was setting up his dreaded war engines, the Roman soldiers noticed—as time passed—a strange phenomenon among the besieged. Once a week all activity ceased. No arrow was fired, no stone hurled. Pompey was amazed to learn that the weekly paralysis was due to respect for the Sabbath. Every Saturday the attackers redoubled their efforts, for there was no fear of retaliation on that day. A short time later the Roman general was victorious.

From the moment the legions entered Jerusalem, Pompey became impatient. The sanctuary was within his grasp. Fed on countless rumours about the secret rites of the Jews, his imagination was ablaze. Pompey entered the Temple, followed by his officers, then crossed the threshold of the Holy of Holies. He was in the most isolated spot where, under Jewish law, only the High Priest was permitted to enter once a year on the Day of Atonement. Pompey did not believe what he saw. 'There was no statue of any divinity inside the Temple. The precinct was empty and no one was carrying out any rite there,' wrote the historian Tacitus later.

*   *   *

But there was no one there to explain to the victorious general the mystical importance of his act. Neither Pompey, nor his officers, nor anyone at Rome would ever understand the profound significance of the sacrilege. Only the Jews knew that in entering the Holy of Holies, Pompey struck at the heart of the Jewish people.

In the first century the Jewish people were not a nation founded on the Graeco-Roman ideal nor, *a fortiori*, a nation in the present-day sense of the term, with an individual history and its natural interests to defend. The Jewish people believed they were chosen by God, as a 'kingdom of priests and a holy people.' Moreover, the Holy of Holies and, by extension, the entire Temple and Jerusalem itself were not a capital city, a national symbol, a seat of government, but a place in which the Divine Presence was manifest. Thus one of God's names retained by Jewish tradition is *Makom*, which is a Hebrew word meaning place, spot, particular point.

The entire Jewish nation, whether still within the limits of the Land of Canaan which had been promised and given by God to the Jews, or dispersed throughout the Graeco-Roman Empire, consequently considered the Holy of Holies as the point at which their own history and divine power converged. The Holy of Holies was the site of the confrontation between God and His people. Pompey's act was not only a sacrilege; for a time it actually interrupted the communication between Israel and its Creator. Pompey's innocent intervention was to trigger off an entirely new chain of events which would soon lead to another conquest of Jerusalem and the dispersion, on a large scale, of the people of the Jews.

This people already willed itself to be irreducible to the other nations of the earth. It stressed its intimacy with God, and its particular role in the midst of humanity.

In reply to the question 'Who is your God?' the early Jews, who received the Torah from Moses, said without a doubt 'He who led us out of Egypt, from the house of bondage.' In this way they affirmed at one and the same time the historical nature of God, His intervention in man's history, and His affiliation to a chosen people, and to them alone. The Jewish religion is therefore founded on an historical God who shatters the natural order of things by intervening in favour of the people He has chosen. The first of these material acts of God in favour of His people was the legendary parting of the waters of the Red Sea which, thirteen hundred years before the Christian era, allowed the Hebrews to enter into their national history.

So the God of Israel is the God of history, liberating man from the domination of nature. Seen from the point of view of nature, man is only one stage, a pawn in the universe. From the historical point of view man, the divine creature, is the supreme being. Moreover, the Jewish religion is inconceivable outside the context of a particular people chosen by God to fulfil His law.

The continuation of the Jewish social unit is therefore absolutely indispensable to the survival of Judaism as a religion. There are no Jews without Judaism, there is no Judaism without Jews. Judaism is therefore a practical religion, made for material beings and not for apprentice gods. Life is the most precious possession. The Jews consciously fear death to the precise extent to which, if it were to touch all the people, it would indicate the end of Judaism and, consequently, the end of the Divine plan for humanity.

In the case of the Jew, morality is not individual, it involves the entire nation. Jewish monotheism effectively leaves the individual ignorant about salvation. Despite the fact that individual merit is indispensable to the continuation of Jewish society, it has no influence on the fulfilment of God's plan. All humanity must be saved, and it can only be saved by its collective merit. In the last resort, the number of individual sinners is of little importance. What counts is that both Jewish history and the history of humanity progress in obedience to the simple laws of their own survival. Thus the Messiah, who is to destroy the barriers between God and man, may perfectly well appear among a generation consisting entirely of sinners. Nowhere so much as in the Jewish conception does God leave His creature in absolute ignorance of the final ideal, in the meaning of creation, in the last word of the human adventure. The Jew, therefore, finds in the Law no other ideal to which he is able to conform than that of the material society involved in history, and of which he is an organic part. This explains the angry Jewish response whenever society is threatened with slavery. Judaism contains the cult of the collective. The love of the people, the love of all men, is a commandment. Judaism trusts in God for whatever else is necessary.

When the Hebrews were slaves in Egypt, they constituted a people with a common origin and destiny. It was for this reason that Pharaoh kept them in a common condition, which affected them all, that of slavery. The Hebrews were forced to do heavy construction. They must have contributed enormously to the building of the pyramids, the monumental tombs of the Pharaohs.

When they had crossed the Red Sea, the Hebrews progressively organized themselves into a society with its laws, its taboos, its structures and, above all, its God. When they had spent forty years wandering in the wilderness of Sinai in search of their being, they entered the Land of Canaan and had to confront other nations and other societies. From this time forward, those who called themselves Jews became a nation, a group of men united by a common culture and a common destiny.

But in keeping with its vocation, this nation was historical, and was in opposition to nature. As a national, historic and anti-natural religion, Judaism did not seek to possess a land. The Promised Land, in the very conception of the One who promised it, was a place for His people to live, ground on which the happiness of the nation might be assured, but not one of the permanent features of the Jewish ethos. Happiness is not a natural possession, but a historical event which assures the existence of the community and facilitates the study of the Law of God. It is in this sense that the promise of 'a land flowing with milk and honey' is to be understood. The Jewish people need not necessarily therefore turn itself into a state because a nation which is settled on a particular piece of ground must accept, to a decisive degree, the domination of nature. Judaism has no static structure—i.e. that of the state—despite the fact that it is a national religion.

But Judaism is not pure spirituality, either. It keeps the sense of the material. The bond between God and His people is a tangible bond made material by the Law. Of course Judaism was in opposition to idolatry. No object was to be the pretext for any kind of cult. Judaism even went so far as to forbid the figuration of objects, people, animals, stars etc., to the point where artistic creativity was strongly affected by it. But the Law, which is of Divine essence, was materially present in the hearts of the people, and so assured the perpetuation of the Divine presence. The Law was materially protected by the Temple. The point of the Exodus from Egypt, of the Jews' wanderings in the Wilderness, of their conquest of the land of Canaan, was to bring the Temple to the place of God, in other words to the point of the insertion of the Divinity into the world. This place, on Mount Moriah in Jerusalem, was beyond nature. It must be preserved and protected. Only the faithful were to be allowed inside. In it was the Holy of Holies where Divine power lived. Around the Temple the life of the Jewish people was organized, as far as the boundaries of Judaea, and beyond that for all the Jews. For those in the last category there was an obligation to go on pilgrimage three times a year to within the shadow of the Temple at Jerusalem. But in spite of the material nature of the Temple, the Jews did not lose sight of the fact that their God is pure spirit, and that nothing can contain Him. During the consecration of the first Temple, King Solomon recalled the incommensurability of the relationship between God and the creature: 'The heaven and heaven of heavens cannot contain thee, how much less this house that I have builded.' (I *Kings* VIII, 27.)

From the moment they received the Torah to the moment when Solomon built the First Temple (965 BC), the Jews carried the Ark of the Covenant with them, symbolizing the presence of God. Jewish tradition maintains that it was the same Law received on Mount Sinai which was placed in the Holy of Holies of Solomon's Temple. But when Nebuchadnezzar burned and sacked the First Temple, he destroyed and profaned the Ark of the Covenant. When Zerubbabel, who was of the line of David, rebuilt the Temple in 520 BC, at the return from the exile in Babylon, he no longer had anything to put in the Holy of Holies.

Forced apart by the Roman eagle, the gates of Judaea gave way. When the legions entered the Jewish city, the Rome-Jerusalem confrontation began. It was a confrontation which was to last for two hundred years.

*   *   *

The average Jew, living in Jerusalem round about 40 BC, might still hold out hopes for national independence. Rome was in undisputed possession of almost the whole of Asia Minor, but her control of Jerusalem was weak. Of course Antipater, the Idumaean, had succeeded in gaining the confidence of Rome and had himself appointed *procurator* of Judaea by Julius Caesar. Antipater had tried to impose his authority by installing his son Herod as Governor of Galilee and his other son Phasael as Governor of Jerusalem. The High Priest, Hyrcanus II, was Antipater's creature, devoid of political power and at the mercy of a decree from the usurper. All that was true, but in the city of Jerusalem, round the Temple and in the markets, travellers talked. Every sort of rumour sustained hopes of the restoration of the Hasmonaeans. This Jewish dynasty was both priestly and political, and had given the Jews independence for eighteen years— from 165 to 143 BC—when they had defeated the Syrian troops of Antiochus Epiphanes. A century later the Hasmonaeans were, for the

Jews, the very incarnation of legitimacy. They were the only ones whose authority and competence could assemble in the hands of one person both priestly and political power—being at the same time both King and High Priest—and reconcile Israel and the modern world by putting the Divine seal on the Jewish national existence through the regular functioning of the High Priesthood.

The average Jew of the period knew vaguely that Mattathiah Antigonus, the last of the Hasmonaeans, was alive and at liberty. But the news of his alliance with Parthians, after the failure of his efforts to convince the Romans of the justice of his cause, gave a new dimension to the dream of a Jewish recovery. The Parthians were an independent people who had resisted the Romans for centuries and blocked their road to Asia. If the news were true, if Mattathiah Antigonus, allied with the Parthians, were really marching on Jerusalem, then Phasael the Idumaean would not count for much in the battle for Jerusalem. The Roman legions at his disposal would not be able to retain control in the face of attack from the outside and revolt from the inside by the Jews in Jerusalem. Indeed, the aristocracy and the people, united against Antipater, increased their demonstrations and blows against authority.

At the end of the day, when the news arrived that Mattathiah Antigonus and the Parthians had arrived under the walls of the city, Jerusalem met once again with her old dream of national independence and national liberty.

The fight was violent but brief. The Jews and Parthians lost heavily, but the Roman legions were put to flight, taking with them those who had collaborated; and foremost among these was Herod. The Governor of Galilee had acted cautiously during the fighting, so he was able to flee easily. On the other hand his brother Phasael, so as not to be thought a coward, preferred to kill himself by being the first to beat his head against a wall.

Popular enthusiasm knew no bounds. Thanksgivings were offered in the Temple. The Parthians were welcomed in the streets of Jerusalem and Antigonus' men enjoyed their first hours of rest after several months of campaigning.

The next day Antigonus was proclaimed King of the Jews. Surrounded by his officers and followed by a large crowd of Jews and Parthians, he solemnly mounted the steps of the royal palace. All knew that a King of Israel who was a descendant of the Hasmonaeans might also be High Priest. Antigonus ordered that Hyrcanus, the High Priest installed

by the usurper, be brought to him. He tore the insignia of the High
Priesthood from his cloak and put them on himself: then the king threw
himself on Hyrcanus, knocked him to the ground and bit the priest's ear
off. Everyone understood what this meant: Antigonus did not want
Hyrcanus to be able to seek the honour of the High Priesthood of Israel
in any circumstances. The person who presided over the religious destinies
of the Jews had to be physically pure, with no bodily defect whatsoever.

*   *   *

Once he was crowned king, Antigonus had few illusions about the mission of the person who reigned over the Jewish people. He knew that at its
origin, Jewish society as Moses had defined it did not need a monarch.
God was the lord, and His authority might be assured by what today we
would call a clergy. As soon as Israel entered into relationships with
other peoples, especially those it had to fight to safeguard its independence,
Israel appointed a leader whose task was both to ensure the safety of the
people and to facilitate God's service.

From then on Israel had to have a national territory. In fact the
safety of Israel might only be satisfactorily assured within well defined
geographical limits. When Israel gave itself a king, it founded a state sited
on its own territory.

But in choosing Jerusalem as his capital, King David—and particularly his son, King Solomon, in building the Temple which bore his
name—introduced the principle of the extra-territorial nature of Israel.
Jerusalem and the Temple were not so much material objects to protect,
as the giving of a material nature to the relationship between Israel and
God, a point of election for the Chosen People. Therefore the kings of
Israel by no means limited their role to that of leaders in war, but justified themselves only if they were high priests as well. The Jews did not
accept a separation of the temporal and the spiritual. Antigonus knew
that in restoring the Hasmonaeans to the throne in his person the Jews
were giving back to the Jewish nation its classic structure in time of war—
monarchy.

Antigonus also knew that not everyone liked the idea of both spiritual
power and temporal authority being vested in the hands of one person.
Opposition to the divine origin of monarchy was not overt during his reign,
but when Rome subsequently wanted to impose either a foreign king or a
Jewish king who was held to be unworthy to hold priestly office, opposition

broke out openly, and the most famous of Judaism's politico-religious parties, the Pharisees, displayed its opposition and its preference for a theocracy; in other words, a society governed directly by God. In the eyes of the Pharisees it was better to have a foreign overlord and religious liberty than a king, chosen by the foreigner among the Jews, who pretended to ascend the throne of David and carry on all the spiritual and political power attached to the dignity of King of the Jews. In any case, whether they were dominated by the Romans or placed under the authority of a usurper, the Jews chose a theocratic social organization that put them beyond the world but ensured their salvation.

For the Pharisees, any sovereignty and any authority ought to be put in the hands of God. Antigonus knew that too, but since the time of the prophets God had been silent. He was unable to exercise His authority directly over Israel, that is why He had made His will known by the Law which He had given. It was this Law which governed Jewish society and which founded the Jewish political system.

*　　　*　　　*

But the Law could not foresee all, nor allow for every eventuality. In order to apply the Law there had to be an authority capable of interpreting it. Moses himself had, on God's orders called together an assembly of seventy just men of Israel to take the important decisions and to govern the people. Moses had complained to God that he was isolated in his capacity as leader. In *Numbers* XI, 16 and 17 it was written: 'And the Lord said unto Moses: Gather unto me seventy men of the elders of Israel whom thou knowest to be the elders of the people and officers over them; and bring them unto the tabernacle of the congregation, that they may stand there with thee. And I will come down and talk with thee there: and I will take of the spirit which is upon thee, and will put it upon them; and they shall bear the burden of the people with thee, that thou bear it not thyself alone.'

The most ancient Jewish memory of such an assembly went back to a century after the return from Babylon, when Ezra and Nehemiah, with a view to a complete renewal of Jewish religion and the Jewish nation, called a large assembly of one hundred and twenty members. Its chief task was to promote knowledge and the Law among the people, and to develop affection for the religion of the fathers.

Antigonus always admired his ancestor John Hyrcanus, not only because he regained Judaea's independence from the Syrians, but also because a century and a half previously he decided to re-establish a large assembly which would be religious, judicial, legislative, political and administrative. This assembly was known as the Sanhedrin. Antigonus attached the utmost importance to this institution and the guarantee it assured. The Sanhedrin was always presided over by a prince who was the mouthpiece of the assembly of the king, the nation and the people. There were two vice-presidents, one responsible for the tribunal and matters of civil and penal justice, and the other was the most learned member of the assembly who was responsible for religious matters. The High Priest, the highest in spiritual matters, was not automatically a member of the Sanhedrin but might, in some circumstances, be called to be its president. There were seventy-one members of the Sanhedrin to comply with tradition. The first assembly had had seventy members and Moses made seventy-one. They were drawn from the learned and wise men who were trusted by the Jewish ascendancy and whose moral integrity and physical perfection was absolute.

*   *   *

While Antigonus restored the traditional institutions of Judaism, Herod, who had fled with the Romans, was in Rome. His reputation both as a zealous administrator in the service of Rome and as a cruel man had preceded him. He was an Idumaean, and only paid lip service to the fact that he was a Jew. He respected the Jewish Law when he was in Jerusalem, but he erected altars to the gods of Rome in the province which he governed. This theological pluralism pleased Rome. Herod knew perfectly well that he had no chance at all of defeating Antigonus' followers on his own. The Jews hated the Idumaean, who was in any case a tool of the Romans, looking after Rome's interest as if he himself were born of a patrician family. To seize power and overthrow Antigonus, Herod would not only have to convince the Romans of his allegiance and loyalty— which was in any case easy enough for him, because of his experience in ruling Galilee—but also show them that the freedom the Jews enjoyed was prejudicial to the interest of Rome and the *pax romana*. He succeeded in persuading Mark Antony that a free Judaea, ruled by a man descended from the family who had defeated the Hellenized Syrians would, in turn, diminish the power of Rome. Was it not in any case a *fait accompli*? Antigonus, allied with the Parthians, had retaken Jerusalem, and pretended to have re-established in its totality the first glory and the total liberty of the kingdom of Israel? Mark Antony was all powerful in Rome at this moment. He recalled the difficulties he had encountered while in Judaea, and convinced the Senate to appoint Herod King of Judaea—and according to Rome Judaea comprised not only Jerusalem and Hebron, but also Galilee, Samaria, the bordering plain with Syria and Egypt, and the east bank of the Jordan and Idumaea, which extended to the south between the Dead Sea and the Mediterranean.

For the first time the Senate decided to impose a non-legitimate ruler, and to demote a king whom the Romans knew to be legitimate. But Antigonus still had to be dislodged. It took Herod—with the help of two Roman legions and Syrian and Idumaean troops—three years to capture Jerusalem. After four months of siege, the would-be king was no further forward, and the defenders of Jerusalem were still holding out. Mark Antony was obliged to send one of his best generals in an attempt to break Jewish resistance in 37 BC.

*   *   *

When Antigonus heard that Mark Antony had decided to give Herod assistance, his first reaction was not to strengthen the garrison at Jerusalem and mobilize more men. He realized that the forthcoming battle would not only be a military battle. To survive an inevitable subjection to Rome, in which Herod would be an accomplice, the Jews would need sacred institutions which the Romans would not dare touch. It did not matter if Antigonus had to disappear, or if an upstart ascended the throne of Israel, but what had to be avoided at all cost was the disappearance of the Jewish nation. The only way, the only restraint, would be the Law and the institutions which devolved from it. Rather than prepare himself for war, Antigonus called together the Elders and redefined before them the functions of the Sanhedrin, and in particular its nature as guarantor of the purity of the priests of Israel.

The Sanhedrin possessed genealogical tables on which were inscribed all the priestly families of Israel, as well as several lay families, both in Judaea and in the Diaspora, who wanted to confirm the authenticity of their origin. It was a highly sought after honour to be entered in the registers.

In addition the Sanhedrin had to control the suitability for office of the priestly families.

'The Sanhedrin sat in the Hall of Carved Stone [in the Temple] and inspected the priests. Those with a bodily defect or blemish contracted by one of their ancestors were forbidden at the altar and went away very sad. Those for whom there was no reason for exclusion, however, were very happy.' (*Talamud*, Kiddushim 76.)

The Sanhedrin also had to oversee the ceremonies held in the Temple. On the eve of the Day of Atonement, delegates from the Sanhedrin went to the High Priest to recall what ceremonies were to be observed. They asked him not to change any of the practices hallowed by tradition.

In addition the Sanhedrin was responsible for decreeing the addition of a thirteenth month to the Hebrew calendar. This calendar was based on the lunar month of thirty days, but every five years an extra month had to be added to re-establish the solar rhythm. This is how the Sanhedrin announced the necessity of adding a thirteenth month:

'Rabbi Gamaliel and the Elders were seated on the step of the Temple Mount and before them was Johanan the scribe. They ordered him to write as follows: "To our brothers the exiles of Babylon, the exiles of Media, of Greece, and the exiles of Israel from all the other countries. May your salvation increase. I tell you that the ewes are still weak, that the chickens are young, that the time of maturity is still not yet come. It has therefore pleased me, as likewise my colleagues, to add to this year thirty days".' (*Talamud*, Sanhedrin 116.)

In a general way, it was also part of the religious duties of the Sanhedrin to judge the woman suspected of adultery and to see that the obligation placed on the king to copy out Deuteronomy was carried out. Finally, the Sanhedrin was the supreme authority for interpretation of the Law. It determined the sense of the difficult passages. It was the only representative of the oral tradition, and its interpretation was the only authentic one and was authoritative.

The Sanhedrin was a court of appeal for all matters in which ordinary judges were declared incompetent. It dealt with false prophets. The crime of idolatry or crimes and offences committed by the high priests were to be heard by the Sanhedrin, and this was also true of the crime of apostasy when committed by a whole town.

In spite of the sacred and unalterable nature of the Torah, the Sanhedrin could have a legislative function. It was empowered to take the necessary steps to preserve the Law in all its purity, in spite of the different circumstances that history imposed on the people of Israel.

In the field of politics and administration, the choice of king and High Priest had to be ratified by the Sanhedrin. It decided whether a war was to be undertaken. The only wars considered obligatory were those which aimed at defeating the Canaanites.

But Antigonus did not hide from himself the fact that, as in all assemblies, the role played by parties decided the issues. Tradition had brought down to him the result of a great miscalculation made by his ancestor, John Hyrcanus. Despite the fact that he was the supreme and uncontested authority of the Jewish nation, Hyrcanus had had difficulties with the Sanhedrin and the Phariseean party. In fact when he re-established the Sanhedrin he had filled it entirely with Pharisees. They were of popular origin and favoured the separation of political power and religious authority. They were loyal to the Scripture and always interpreted it in the social sense and for the general good. But John Hyrcanus, on the perfidious advice of a man called Eleazar ben Poirah, had wanted to test the Pharisee's allegiance to his person. He acted as High Priest and put on the pontifical tiara. A learned Pharisee, Jehuda ben Gedidim, ordered him to remove it. The Pharisee believed that John's mother had been a slave in Modin, the town from which the Hasmonaeans came. The purity of the High Priest could not be put in doubt for any reason whatsoever. The king demanded that the insolent man be condemned. The Sanhedrin, basing itself on the fact that the Torah made no recognition of the crime of *lèse-majesté*, only condemned Gedidim to corporal punishment and prison. John Hyrcanus was furious at the resistance of the Pharisaic doctors, drove them all out of the Sanhedrin and replaced them with Sadducees—the noble priestly party—who were conservative and favourable to the established order.

Antigonus decided to restore all power to the Pharisees.

*   *   *

Jerusalem was not completely besieged. There was feverish activity in Herod's camp. Roman power had made him King of Judaea, but because of Antigonus he was unable to conquer his capital. Out of political calculation, and for love, Herod had just repudiated his Idumaean wife Doris. He then married Mariamne, a Hasmonaean princess and half-cousin to Antigonus. Herod thought that this marriage would win him the favour of the Jews, and that in any case his descendants would be regarded as authentic successors to King David. Mariamne was very beautiful, dark, tall and delicate. She fascinated the Idumaean. Of course Herod would have preferred the marriage to be celebrated in Jerusalem after the victory. But he wanted this marriage so much that he could not make it depend on the outcome of the battle.

When, on the day appointed, Mariamne arrived in the Roman camp surrounded by her father and her brothers, wearing a huge veil which almost entirely covered her, the Romans drawn up to attention on either side of the narrow pathway made noises of admiration. Herod was dressed in red and wore a Roman helmet. He was small but stood erect, his face lifeless and his blue eyes devoid of all expression. Surrounded by his body-guard he advanced. There were no priests to solemnize the wedding, but the Jews did not need them. Marriage is a contract between the couple, a sacrament. For Mariamne to become his wife Herod had only to say in front of two witnesses the words hallowed by tradition 'Behold you are betrothed to me, according to the Law of Moses and of Israel.' Then all present thanked God for having created the universe to proclaim His glory, for having made man in His image and His likeness.

A few years later Herod was to murder with his own hands the wife he had married. But his love for her was always genuine. At the end of his days Herod ran through the palace shouting the name Mariamne, the most noble and most beautiful of the Jewish princesses.

*   *   *

Singing and dancing went on until dawn rose from behind the mountains of Moab, and the sounds of the festivities even reached the people besieged in Jerusalem.

Inevitably the celebration ended and the Roman war machine moved into motion; soon the soldiers had mounted an attack. Once more Jerusalem was to feel the weight of battle. The first line of Jewish defence was broken and the crack Roman troops penetrated the city. Again, it was towards the Temple that the last survivors gravitated. Soldiers mixed with armed priests, who celebrated the sacrifices between bouts of fighting. The Romans broke through the outer wall of the Temple and occupied the Court of the Gentiles. There they stopped, leaving to Herod's men the task of entering the sacred area where Gentiles were forbidden to go.

Night fell quickly and halted war operations while the besieged mounted guard around the *ner tamid*—the perpetual or eternal flame which was never allowed to go out. Slowly the priests took off their vestments, the linen trousers, the white tunic, the belt and the cap. They rolled them up carefully and then stretched out in the alcoves on the ground, their faces turned towards the flame. Other priests went round to ensure that the Temple gates were tightly closed. But when dawn lit up the horizon, no one dreamed of opening up the outer gates. So the Romans broke them down, allowing the Idumaean troops to deliver the final assault that would make them masters of Jerusalem for the greater glory of their leader Herod, son of Antipater, acknowledged King of the Jews by the Roman Senate.

Before seizing Antigonus, the new king had the members of the Sanhedrin who were guilty of having invested the last of the Hasonaeans put to death. But Herod was too clever to covet the High Priesthood. He did not take up the pontifical vestments or the tiara. He knew the Jewish laws, and he did not see himself for a single moment as the High Priest, the one who, in the name of the Jewish people, entered the Holy of Holies once a year.

As for the Romans, they took Antigonus prisoner and had already begun to prepare Mark Antony's triumph. They were pleased at the idea of having a new Oriental king to add colour to their procession. But Herod rushed to the Roman General, and spoke in favour of Antigonus. Having expressed his admiration for the invincibility of Rome, he pointed out that Antigonus was a very insignificant king and unworthy of appearing in a triumph of any importance. Antigonus had only reigned for a few months and could hardly be considered a monarch, since he had been crowned by Jews in revolt, whereas he, Herod, was already acknowledged King of Judaea by the illustrious Roman Senate. The victorious general was convinced by the argument and handed the unfortunate Antigonus over to Herod, who had him taken to Caesarea at once. The whole operation was intended to prevent Antigonus from having any direct contact with the Romans. Herod knew his protectors well. He knew that they were capable of responding to a just cause, and of being moved by the sort of arguments that Antigonus might advance: for example that of the end of a dynasty.

While Mark Antony triumphed in Rome, Herod beheaded Mattathiah Antigonus, the last King-High Priest of Israel.

*   *   *

Herod did not think that by executing Antigonus he had damaged the principles upon which Jewish society rested. He hoped to re-establish the normal functioning of institutions, particularly the Temple at Jerusalem. He planned to restore to the sanctuary its former splendour. He also wanted to give back to Jerusalem its old lustre, and to rebuild the monuments that were its glory.

Herod, who had devoted his energies to breaking Jewish legitimacy, wanted to give back to the people the very symbol of national independence by decorating, enlarging and remodelling the Temple of Zerubbabel. For seventeen years he nursed the project.

There were three models at Herod's disposal; the Temple of Solomon, the Temple of Zerubbabel, which had been seriously damaged in the course of the recent fighting, and the model in Ezechiel's vision—the Temple of modern times which he described in his prophecy when exiled in Babylon. But Herod's project only made sense if he had the consent of the clergy, and the mistrust that he inspired in people was a serious obstacle. And as far as religious matters were concerned, distrust turned to positive repulsion at everything that emanated from the upstart. For instance, the new plans would entail the admission of workmen to the Temple of Zerubbabel, which in spite of the recent destruction still continued to fulfil its role as the point of contact with the Divinity. Might not this be simply a new trick on Herod's part to destroy the Temple once and for all?

During the years leading up to the announcement of his plans for the Temple, round about 20 BC, Herod had already built several structures to ensure his glory—in particular a magnificent royal palace with four towers. The palace dominated the entire upper city and its style of architecture revealed the King's concern for security. Herod had also enlarged and embellished the fortress on the Temple Mount and, in honour of Mark Antony, had named it the Antonia. One of the four towers of the Antonia made the task of watching the Temple a simple matter.

Once he had taken these precautions, Herod was free to consider restoring the Temple to its former glory. Reassured by his architectural genius, the Jews accepted the idea that the king really did want to beautify the Temple. Nevertheless, they laid down a number of conditions in return for their acceptance. The first was that unclean hands might have no part in holy work. Herod agreed, and had more than a thousand priests instructed in masonry and carpentry. The second condition was that nothing was to be destroyed before the material for its replacement had been assembled. Herod also agreed to this, and accepted all the other conditions laid down by the clergy for the completion of the work.

In common with the Temple of Solomon, the Temple of Zerubbabel, built when the first exiles returned from Babylon, was on Mount Moriah at Jerusalem. On this site Abraham had agreed to sacrifice his son Isaac before God's intervention stayed his hand. When King David built his own palace at Jerusalem, it seemed abnormal to the people—and to the king himself—that God should continue to live in the Ark of the Tabernacle, in other words practically in a tent. David therefore decided to build in Jerusalem a house for God, which would prove that the people of Israel were from now on installed with their God in a definite country and that their wanderings were over.

Israel's worship of God was sacrificial. Until the Torah was given, sacrifices might take place anywhere, preferably on a high place. In this way, Abel, Cain, Noah and the Patriarchs had offered sacrifices to a God who had revealed Himself before He made His will known. As soon as Moses had codified the Law, the offering of sacrifices was made obligatory 'before the door of the Tabernacle,' in other words at the entrance to the Ark of the Covenant, the place where God met His people.

David therefore wanted to establish the Tabernacle definitely on Mount Moriah and build the Temple on this site, where the people could sacrifice to their God. But it fell to his son Solomon to have the honour of building the Temple. Since he was not worthy enough, David had to content himself with greeting the Temple from afar. The reunion of the portable temple which accompanied the Jews during their Exodus with the spot where God ordered Abraham to sacrifice his son marks the beginning of the temple cult, the central institution of national Judaism. When almost a thousand years later Herod began to reconstruct the sanctuary of Israel, he was well aware of the imperatives to which he had to adhere in order to preserve the purity of the spot, maintain its organization for receiving sacrifices and, as far as possible, draw to himself the thanks of the Jewish people.

The great enterprise began in 20 BC and was only entirely finished long after Herod's death, round about AD 60. But the major part of the work was finished in 9 BC, when Herod was still alive.

*   *   *

Two men reached the summit of the Mount of Olives. One was old and

short of breath. He was wearing the traditional costume of the Jerusalem
Jews. The other was very young. He was pushing onwards, and anxious to
see the panorama from the top. He was wearing Greek clothes, but was a
Jew, like the old man who was his uncle.

It was the young man's first visit to Jerusalem. He had lived in
Athens all his life, the town that was the beacon of civilization. From the
top of the Mount of Olives his eye spotted the sanctuary Herod had built.
The first thing he noticed was the Temple platform. It was made of white
stone covered with gold. In the rays of the sun the Temple shone strangely
as if the reflections from the stone and the gold were combining to out-
shine all other lights and all other colours. The pilgrim also noticed the
gilded spikes placed at regular intervals round the terrace. He asked questions of his uncle, who had never left the Holy City. The spikes were
designed to keep the birds off the sacred building since they might defile
it. The Temple esplanade seemed immense to someone who came to
Jerusalem for the first time. Its surface area was twice the size of the
Acropolis in Athens, which was the pride of Greek civilization. The old
man said that because of the underpinning Herod had carried out, the
ground area of Zerubbabel's Temple had been doubled.

The two men began their descent to the sanctuary. Every step provided a different impression of the building. As they reached the bottom
of the Valley of Kedron the colours of the Temple seemed to get darker,
but when they reached the very foot of Mount Moriah, Herod's Temple
was bathed in white light, as if it were covered in snow. The outer wall
rose very straight and very high, in a sheer drop. In the past, this was
known as the pinnacle. Another striking feature was the size of the stones
used for the wall, some of which measured twenty-four cubits—that is,
about forty feet. The stone of Jerusalem is pink, and varies according to
the time of day, from off white to pitch black. The old man said that it
was as common in Jerusalem as gold in the time of the kings. The stones
were put one on top of the other in twenty-five layers to form the outer
wall.

As he passed through the Susa Gate, one of the eight gates of the
Temple, the young man was filled with an emotion which came from the
very depths of his memory. It had the intonation of the Jewish soul
common to all Jews when the Temple is involved. When they entered
the Court of the Gentiles, an immense market place similar to those he
knew in Greek cities, they saw tradesmen, unarmed soldiers, women,
children, and particularly Romans, Egyptians and Greeks. There were

animals on display, and moneychangers scrupulously counting their money. The conversations he heard against a background of children's and tradesmen's cries were concerned with news from the Roman Empire and the celebrations that had taken place at Caesarea when King Herod visited it.

They were jostled on all sides and occasionally engulfed by groups of people who had gathered around various preachers. Finally they reached the steps which led to the holy precinct. It was an esplanade six cubits higher than the Court of the Gentiles, where non-Jews were excluded on penalty of death. A stone wall about three cubits high divided the two areas. No Gentile might pass it. At intervals was placed an inscription in Latin and Greek which read: 'It is forbidden for any foreigner to cross the wall and to enter the area of the sanctuary. Whoever is apprehended will himself be responsible for his death which will follow.'

But these two men were Jews, and they were therefore able to enter the Court of the Women. This area was not exclusively for women; Jewish men could naturally go there. But the women could go no closer to the altar than this court. It was an area 136 cubits (310 feet) long and was a plinth for the Temple. The holy area began with the Court of the Women. It had nine gates, four to the north, four to the south and one to the east. The two men passed through this last gate, which was far and away the most beautiful. There were five steps. At wide intervals the pilgrim noticed collecting boxes like inverted trumpets on which the women could leave their offerings, though they were not allowed to go further.

The two men now crossed the entry to the Court of Israel, the third concentric zone. Only Jewish men were allowed there. The Court of Israel was seven cubits higher than the Court of the Women. The men passed through this last, imposing gate, which was known as Nikanor's Gate, in memory of a rich donor settled in Alexandria. This area was much smaller than the others. But from it the men were able to see clearly what was taking place in the Court of the Priests, where the sacrifices were made. Only the 'Cohens', who prepared the sacrifice, were allowed into the Court of the Priests, and then only on condition that they were in a state of perfect purity. Once a year, on the anniversary of the giving of the law to Moses, the people were allowed into the Court of the Priests and went around the altar seven times while the High Priest sprinkled the faithful with water. This was taking place today. The old man, still leading his nephew, was the first one to enter the place where the very heart of Israel

beat, and where the altar of sacrifice stood. This was a vast cube thirty
cubits square and five cubits high. A ramp led up to it.

Twice a day the High Priest or his representatives, having laid hands
on the animals for sacrifice, had them killed and sprinkled the altar of the
Temple with their blood. The blood ran through a system of canals to the
Valley of the Kedron.

Blood was considered the fundamental source of life. Through the
process of aspersion earthly life joined the life that was in God, so as to
mingle in one vital element the source of all power. Sacrifices were made
twice daily in the name of Israel, and did not exclude private sacrifices
that each individual might have made in his name by a sacrificer—as an
act of thanksgiving, for the redemption of his sins, or on the occasion of
the death of a dear one, or finally as an offering for purification. The
Temple was the scene of perpetual sacrifice throughout the day.

There were not only blood sacrifices. Flowers, vegetables, wine and
oil might be offered to God, and incense was believed to be equally
agreeable to Him.

The two pilgrims now reached the sacred spot where no animal
sacrifice was offered. They were forbidden to enter. Even so they could see
the altar of incense, the table of the shewbread and the famous seven-
branched candelabrum, which was made of solid gold and had been
chosen by Antigonus as the symbol of national independence. Above the
Court of the Priests the young man noticed a long gallery running right
round the building, with carved doors opening off it. That was where the
famous Hall of Carved Stone was, where the Sanhedrin met. There were
other rooms for the priests and for storing ceremonial objects. But the
treasure of Israel was not here. Only the treasurer had access to it in the
vaults, where, over the centuries, fabulous riches had accumulated. All
sorts of precautions were taken since Crassus, in 54—about half a century
earlier—ransacked the Jews' possessions from top to bottom. It was not
surprising that the Temple contained great riches. For generations all the
Jews in the inhabited world, from Europe and Asia, had contributed
generously to Temple funds.

But all the priests turned round and knelt towards the eastern side
of the building, where the Holy of Holies was situated. The old man and
his nephew saw only a vast curtain woven with threads of four different
colours representing the four elements. When the High Priest arrived
there was a burst of singing and trumpets rang out. Slowly the Chief
Priests of Israel crossed the holy place then stopped at the entrance to

the portico from where he was to bless the assembled people:
'May the Lord bless you and keep you, may the Lord cause His face to
shine upon you and be gracious unto you, may He lift up His countenance
unto you and give you His peace.'

Like a huge wave, the voice of the kneeling people rose and they
all replied: 'Blessed be His name, whose glorious kingdom is for ever
and ever.'

Now the young man understood that the Temple was a universal
organization, and that there was a place for everyone in it. The foreigner
might enter the Court of the Gentiles and share in the life of Israel. But
woe betide him, all the same, if he took it upon himself to enter the part
reserved for the women of Israel. And the women, for their part, could
watch the sacrifices from their court, but might not enter the Court of
Israel, which was for the laymen. As for the people as a whole, they
could not enter the Court of the Priests, who were themselves divided
into three. The Levites organized the worship, and the Cohens carried
out the sacrifices. The High Priest was unique. But the most illustrious
inhabitant of the Temple was God Himself, who lived in the Holy of
Holies. Because nothing was able to contain God, Jewish tradition did
not put Him in the Holy of Holies but His name. God's names were
infinite and innumerable, but one of them concerned Israel. By giving of
one of His names God made Himself known specifically to Israel. That
was the name which dwelt in the Holy of Holies.

The two men were once more in the Court of the Gentiles. They both
still felt the emotion aroused in them when the High Priest blessed the
whole of Israel. As they mingled with the crowd of Jews and non-Jews,
the pilgrims best understood the reason for this point of contact between
Israelites and Gentiles which was so close to the meeting place between
Israel and its God. Israel had to be at one both with God and the rest of
humanity.

Slowly the two men melted into Jerusalem. They disappeared into the
midst of people like themselves, carrying away with them the image of
the Temple in which God dwelt, and the conviction that the independence
of Israel would soon be achieved.

*   *   *

Herod was relaxed. He was little troubled by the worship or the daily
sacrifices in the Temple. The benefit of religion was that it made the

people forget their unhappiness and encouraged them to hope for a better life through prayer, and not revolution. There were a few subversive speeches made in the outer courts of the sanctuary, but they did not cause him much worry, either. He thought that the Temple he had given Israel would prevent the Jews from taking up the theories of the preachers who talked about earthly paradise and rebellion. In any case his spies would be sure to let him know of any real danger. Herod thought that it would be quite enough to execute one or two bellicose preachers from time to time so as to have some peace. After all, the Jews in Jerusalem were poorly armed by comparison with his own Idumaean or Arab troops who were Jewish in part, to say nothing of the strong Roman legion encamped at Caesarea, or of the formidable Syrian army only two days' march from Jerusalem.

Nevertheless, three times a year Herod was distinctly alarmed. The worship of the Temple was binding on all Jews whether they lived in Jerusalem or Judaea, whether they lived in the Roman Empire or east of the Euphrates. Every year, on three different occasions, the Diaspora of Israel had to go to the Temple at Jerusalem. These were the days of pilgrimage.

The most important was the Passover, which commemorated the Exodus from Egypt. It was both a religious and a national day, since after the Exodus from Egypt, Israel met its God and then became a nation. During the celebration of the Passover, the Pascal lamb was sacrificed. It was the most ancient of the sacrifices the Israelites made to their God. Even when they were in Egypt the Hebrews had sacrificed a lamb when the spring came.

The second feast of pilgrimage was Pentecost, which fell seven weeks after the Passover, and was therefore celebrated at the end of spring. It commemorated the gift of the Torah which God made to Israel through Moses. Every Jew had to offer to God on that day the first fruits of his crops. The Ten Commandments were recited before a prostrate crowd: 'I am the Lord your God Who brought you out of Egypt, from the house of bondage. You shall have no other God but Me.'

The third feast of pilgrimage was known as the Feast of Tabernacles, which commemorated the wanderings of Israel and served to remind the nation that they were nomads, without homes, or any seat of hope. The Feast of Tabernacles came at the beginning of autumn, and the last fruits were offered to God.

These celebrations all had an agricultural character and corresponded exactly to the activities of the great majority of the inhabitants of Judaea at the time. The whole nation enthusiastically seized the chance to approach the holy Temple. An enormous crowd invaded the Holy City, coming not only from Palestine, but from the Diaspora which, in the 1st century, accounted for roughly three times as many Jews as there were in Herod's empire. At this time one Roman in ten was a Jew. The contact between Palestinians and people of the Diaspora existed on religious, political, cultural and commercial levels alike. There were a great many pilgrims. As Philo of Alexandria said: 'Innumerable multitudes from cities without number arrive, some by land, some by water, from east and west, north and south, to each one of the feasts.' Some thought they remembered an occasion when three million pilgrims came to Jerusalem. Others even put the number of visitors as high as twelve millions. Pilgrims had many privileges in Jerusalem, and legal protection. Inn keepers, for instance, had the right to ask only for the skin of a sacrificed animal by way of retribution. Nothing else.

These concentrations of believing Jews disturbed not only the Roman soldiers but also Herod. But the King of the Jews did not want to stop the pilgrimages. On the contrary, he made things easier by improving the road from Babylon so that pilgrims could reach Jerusalem in a fortnight. He knew that banning pilgrimages would be interpreted as sacrilege and would incite the Jews to revolt. But such was the national and religious ferment, the excited state of people's minds and the enthusiasm of the pilgrims, that the danger of a nationalist explosion or of religious fanaticism was evident during the celebrations. So Herod increased the number of troops in the Antonia fortress on each occasion. The Roman soldiers left their garrison at Caesarea and camped close to Jerusalem, ready for any eventuality.

*   *   *

Although he was personally responsible for giving the Temple a splendour it had never had before, Herod felt that the sanctuary of Israel was beyond his jurisdiction. Although he had nominated a High Priest loyal to himself, and had a tailor-made Sanhedrin, the organization of the Temple services appeared to obey rules which they did not control.

In fact there were twenty thousand people in the service of the Temple. Similar to civil servants they were paid out of the various types of offerings made. The High Priest, who embodied the sum total of Jewish religion, was at the top of the hierarchy of Temple dignitaries. The Captain of the Temple, the High Priest's assistant, was responsible for the administration and was in command of an armed police responsible for keeping order. Below him were officers in charge of the internal security, defence and order of the Temple.

In addition to the dignitaries there were the priests and Levites. Priests might only marry a virgin or widow of Israel. They were approved for the priesthood by the Sanhedrin and were the real ministers of prayer and the Jewish faith. The Levites did not exercise a priestly function, but rather were responsible for guarding the Temple, watching its doors and providing the choirs.

Finally, there were the treasurers responsible for the general administration, offerings, and the Temple treasure; the porters responsible for policing the doors and making sure that they were opened and closed at the right times, and for forbidding foreigners access to the Temple proper; administrators responsible for the practical organization of the religious ceremonies, and the musicians.

Of course Herod might always have a captain of the Temple dismissed, or a treasurer, but how was he to control the mass of young priests, the recruitment of police, and the sermons preached in every corner of the sanctuary? Herod knew perfectly well that an organization such as this, over which he did not have complete control, was liable to become the centre of revolutionary activity, and that several hundreds of thousands of believers and twenty thousand officials were involved in the Temple's activities.

Herod and his followers could not shut their eyes to reality. They would certainly have been wrong to imagine that the priestly caste indulged only occasionally in intellectual activity or studied the Torah, or that the common people were indifferent to philosophy. For the Jews, theology was itself a revolutionary concept, and although the Temple was a place of worship, it was inconceivable to have a Jewish gathering without some study of the Law. The power of the Sadduceean priests was comparable to the importance of the Pharisees—who were of more popular origin and were increasingly interested in spiritual matters. The Pharisees were intellectuals obsessed with progress, but they were absolutely true to their religion, in the same way that they were zealous for Israeli national independence. This independence was expressed through the freedom of the Temple worship. The Pharisees were therefore both intellectuals from the lower stratum of society, social reformers, religious integrationists and nationalists in the face of Roman occupation. Within the ranks of the Pharisees were the Scribes, in other words the intellectuals, who imagined that the permanence of the life of Israel would be guaranteed by handing the knowledge of Israel on from generation to generation.

The Scribes and Pharisees obviously spent a lot of time in the Temple and gave it an atmosphere which reflected their own preoccupations. They were surrounded by people who studied the Law, commented on it and had a truly political education, founded on the idea of Jewish independence. Herod did everything possible to contain this intellectual activity within limits acceptable to himself.

*   *   *

Rabbi Hillel was neither a prophet nor a priest, nor a temporal ruler of Israel. He was simply the founder of a school and the innovator of a new way of understanding the teaching of the Torah.

In the reign of Herod he was the foremost intellectual master in Israel. Hillel was born in Babylon and, like Moses, lived for a hundred and twenty years. He spent forty years in Babylon, forty years learning, and forty years teaching within the shadow of the Temple. A descendant of the House of David, he was considered the true spiritual head of the national community of Israel.

Hillel taught that poverty was no obstacle to a study of the law, which is why the Pharisees adopted him as their master. He believed that the entire Torah was founded on the moral teaching of Judaism contained in the commandment, 'Love thy neighbour as thyself.' He therefore thought that the love of God came after love of the created thing. He said: 'Do not unto others what you would not have done to yourself; that is the whole of the Torah, the rest is only commentary.'

But every Jew had to study the Law, for according to Hillel an ignorant man was not immune from sin, and nor was he pious. Hillel also said: 'Study where there are masters, teach where there are pupils.'

Hillel gave priority to teaching the moral content of Judaism. Another of his sayings was, 'Do not withdraw yourself from the community,' taking isolation to be bad for the equilibrium of the individual. 'Judge not your neighbour unless you are in his place,' implying that no one person's views can coincide exactly with those of another. 'Never believe in yourself, until the day of your death,' showing that merit is never acquired definitively. 'My humility is my uplifting and my uplifting is my humility,' recalling the insignificance of man before the Divine plan. Finally, 'the man who is tied up in his business will never become wise,' showing that each one should devote himself entirely to the study of the Law. All of Hillel's teaching was directed towards the material presence of God in the heart of His people, and so he said: ' "If I am here," says God, "the whole world is here. If I am not here, no one is here." '

Hillel's teaching, that of 'the gentle and learned one,' was alive in the Temple, in spite of Rabbi Shamaiah, who spread a different teaching which put the accent on the rigour necessary to respect the Law, the definite nature of the judgement of God, and the primacy of divine service. The implied conflict between these two teachings excited the crowds. But Hillel and Shamaiah both had men among their disciples who asked themselves how to use their master's teaching for their planned revolt against Herod and Rome.

*   *   *

These men knew that Herod the Great was approaching the end of his days, that the Temple was increasing in splendour, and that Jewish society was reaching one of the high points of its strength: that society was in fact free to serve its God and give to the teaching of the Torah a degree of popularity that had never been equalled. The Jews were numerous and rich, dispersed throughout the Graeco-Roman world, but turned entirely towards Jerusalem and its Temple. It seemed to them that Jewish society must very shortly fulfil its own ideal. But Roman occupation began to weigh more heavily. Throughout their vast empire, the Romans were adept at adding to their Pantheon the gods of the peoples they had conquered, and they had particular respect for this God of the Jews who forbade the representation on their coins of any human figure. In fact Roman money was not current in Jerusalem, and on various occasions Roman soldiers had had to bypass the city so that the Roman eagle on their helmets would not arouse the anger of its inhabitants. Then again, the Jew of Jerusalem seemed to attach only relative importance to the fact that the administration was in foreign hands—so long as nothing interfered with his own social organization, with his worship and with the infinite respect due to his God.

But people began to realize that the Romans were less indifferent to the organization of the Jewish religion. For instance, they kept the High Priest's vestments in the Antonia fortress as a pledge, and only let them out on the Day of Atonement—in the hope that the Jews would be peaceful for the rest of the year so as to get the holy vestments back. Gradually the Jews who were influenced by progressive young intellectuals became less indifferent to the way in which the Romans conducted public affairs.

From the day the Jews received the Torah at the hands of Moses until the first revolts which marked the beginning of the Great Jewish War against the Romans, Jewish society had undergone many vicissitudes, had seen many disappointments which had threatened both its religious propensities and its national identity; but spiritual power concentrated in the Temple and the need for national autonomy were never greater than at the death of Herod. A people in possession of the Torah, which they regarded as the greatest religious monument ever given to man, could not accept the domination and law of those ignorant of the true God. The Romans had devoted their genius to the possession of an immense empire, without moral scruple—either collective or individual—knowing only the power of the State, indifferent to the search for God, ready to deify emperors, men or animals and to acquire the gods of the nations subject to their rule.

At this point in its existence, the Jewish nation was going to embark on the great adventure of revolt and attempt to drive the Roman invader out of Judaea.

2 Popular Resistance and Messianic Anticipation

Augustus was a simple man, in fact he was small and sickly. He wore woollen garments of cloth woven by his family. He ate little. People went into his presence without formalities, and he saw everyone who had some reason for complaint. The emperor whose name was synonymous with greatness and equity had just heard of the death of Herod the Great, King of Judaea. In a confused sort of way, he felt that Rome would have difficulty in replacing such a servant. He was rather anxious, and wondered whether the death of the Idumaean would not also signify the end of an epoch. The Jews were rebellious by nature and hostile to the very principle of Roman civilization founded on emperor worship. Only Herod had been able to establish a perfect balance between the religious aspirations of those barbarians and their proud concern for national independence. In a reflective state of mind Augustus considered the latest news to have reached him during the last few days from that distant province of Rome which was not truly Roman. Augustus remembered that Herod had had a golden eagle placed at the main entrance of the Temple of the Jews. This was done to honour imperial Rome and to remind the Jews that their independence was limited. But two Jewish ring-leaders—Judas son of Sepphoraeus and Matthias son of Margalus—had encouraged the Jews to tear down the Roman emblem, 'saying that even if danger was involved it was a glorious thing to die for the laws of their country: for those who came to such an end there was a sure hope of immortality . . .' And the rioting crowd brought down the idol 'at mid-day, when masses of people were walking about the Temple courts.' (Josephus, *The Jewish War*.) The leaders of this act were burned alive and their followers beheaded, but in their action the crowds had seen a repetition of what Abraham, the father of their people, had done in overturning the idols of his native town.

Augustus was surprised at himself, for he could not remember devoting such a long period of thought to the Jews and Judaea before. A few days later he learned that Herod's heirs were on their way to ask him to adjudicate between them. Possibly he ought to devote himself more to the question of the succession. Possibly it was indeed the end of an epoch.

A ship under full sail sped towards Rome. An entire royal family was journeying to Augustus for the verification of the will in which Herod drew up a division of his kingdom among those of his children still living: Archelaus, Antipas and Philip.

Naturally Archelaus was there, for the largest share of the kingdom had been promised to him. He was accompanied by his mother and some friends. There was also Salome, the dead king's sister, who in principle had come to demand her share in the inheritance, basically the town of Yabne, but who would not fail to accuse her nephew Archelaus before Augustus of having violated the holy Jewish laws. Antipas also made the journey. He seemed to be able to count on Salome's support. He referred to an older will of Herod's under which he would be sole heir to the kingdom.

While the royal family was sailing to Rome, the situation throughout Judaea was not particularly favourable to Herodian interests. The very day after Herod's funeral celebrations—which had lasted seven days—the people pressed forward with their demands: lower taxes and amnesty for prisoners. Archelaus had agreed to those two items, but he was not ready to agree to call for vengeance for the death of the brave Jews who had taken down the golden Roman eagle. Archelaus was obviously unable to disown his father on the eve of his journey to Rome. Nor could he envisage a revolt in blood in the first hours of the interregnum. Tension was extremely high among the Jews because it was the eve of the Passover, and a crowd was converging on the Temple. Everyone was shouting for vengeance for Judas and Matthias. Archelaus sent more men to dissuade the rioters. 'Their approach infuriated the huge mob, who pelted the cohort with stones and killed most of the men, wounding the tribune, who barely escaped with his life. Then as if nothing strange had occurred they turned to sacrifice.' (*The Jewish War*.)

Gradually the revolutionary spirit of the people was being forged. In retaliation, Archelaus sent in a large force to confront the Jews, and three thousand people were killed. Thus, when Archelaus reached Rome, his hands were already covered with the blood of people he hoped soon to be dominating.

Another source of conflict was greed for control of the Temple treasure. Augustus learned from despatches from Varus, Governor of Syria, that Sabinus, Roman procurator in Judaea, was trying to seize the treasure, and that he was increasing his pressure on the guardians of the Temple. In anger, the people had attacked the Roman garrison on the Day of Pentecost in 4 BC. Sabinus retreated to the tower of Phasael and gave the order to take the Temple, where the angry Jews had once more taken refuge. The Jews were more numerous and their position was better, but the Romans were very experienced in the art of war. They were well entrenched and easily avoided the missiles hurled by their opponents. The Jews then climbed to the top of the Temple gates, from where they rained a torrent of arrows on the Romans. Augustus' legions lost a lot of men. Furthermore, the Romans were unable to counter blow for blow, since the Jews were so high up and the Roman missiles could not harm them. When confronted by such situations the Romans did not hesitate, nor allow their enemies to hold such an advantage, even temporarily. They set fire to the gates without a thought for the beauty or richness of their decoration.

All the Jews in the Temple were either killed in battle or put to flight. The Romans rushed into the Treasury and with Sabinus in the forefront, carried off a large amount of gold. The Jews were furious. Sabinus and the Romans were in turn surrounded in the royal palace. The Jews wanted the treasure back, and promised Sabinus and his men that their lives would be spared if they gave it back, but Sabinus was waiting for the reinforcements promised by the governor Varus. Confident, the greedy Roman decided to hold on. This action influenced the people of Judaea. Groups of men came from all parts of the country, determined to fight their hated enemy.

*   *   *

Judas of Gamala, known as the Galilean, was not a man of war or a revolutionary in the classical mould. He was a distinguished sophist, a philosopher, an intellectual. He probably arrived at the concept of revolt more through his personal situation than through his reflections on the matter. He was the son of Ezechias who was taken prisoner and kept in a state of slavery by Herod when he was Governor of Galilee. Ezechias was himself leader of a band of men who had revolted against authority. When he was taken by Herod's men he was executed without a trial. But when the Sanhedrin heard what Herod had done, they bowed to popular pressure and summoned King Hyrcanus—who was then ruler of Judaea but without real authority—and ordered him to explain himself, and the

Governor of Galilee's crime. Herod arrived, dressed magnificently, and accompanied by a large escort; he was most arrogant and confident because of the support he had from the Romans. He was finally acquitted, and would later have his revenge on the Sanhedrin and the Pharisees who composed it. Judas the Galilean therefore had every reason to revolt, since his father had been put to death by a tyrant, and his murderer acquitted under pressure from Rome.

But it was also the reflective side of his nature which led him to organize the struggle against Rome. He knew the epic of the Maccabees, those intrepid fighters who, 130 years earlier, had succeeded in re-establishing Israeli independence. He knew that if the Jews organized themselves they would be capable of winning back their freedom. Of course he did not pretend to be wearing the mantle of those famous defenders of liberty, the founders of a dynasty, but he knew that their exploits might serve him as a model. Judas the Galilean also knew that God loved those who were full of zeal for the defence of His name. He remembered God's words to Moses in *Numbers* XXV, 11: 'Phinehas, the son of Eleazar, the son of Aaron the priest, hath turned my wrath away from the children of Israel while he was zealous for my sake among them . . .' God was exclusive, His reign absolute and the power of men over men ought to be opposed. God alone reigns. Judas the Galilean also knew that men are not divided into masters and slaves. Men are the slaves of God, but no man will ever be able to rule over another unless he cross the will of God. Judas reproached many of his fellow-countrymen for being 'cowards if they submitted to paying taxes to the Romans, and after serving God alone accepted human masters.' (*The Jewish War*.)

Driven on by his ideal, Judas—having heard that Jerusalem had once more been pillaged by Roman troops—called together his men around Sepphoris in Galilee. He occupied the town, took the arsenal by storm and armed his troops.

*   *   *

Although Augustus was informed about the current military situation in Judaea, he had no idea of the extent to which the climate had deteriorated, and that a revolutionary party had appeared. He had just received fifty Jewish ambassadors who had come to talk to him not of peace or war but about religion: about God, and the special nature of the Jewish people who did not want a king. An astonishing thing was that the eight thousand Jews living in Rome, many of whom were Roman citizens, joined the ambassadors from Judaea to demand reunion with Syria, so as to benefit from direct administration from Rome. This move amazed Augustus and did not help the cause of Archelaus, nor that of Herod's other heirs. The ambassadors from Judaea spoke vehemently against Herod and the Herodians.

'When the accusers were called upon they first went through Herod's crimes, declaring that it was not to a king that they had submitted but to the most savage tyrant that had ever lived ... Depriving them of their old prosperity and their ancestral laws he had reduced his people to poverty and utter lawlessness. In fact the Jews had endured more calamities at Herod's hands in a few years than their ancestors had endured in all the time since they left Babylon in the reign of Xerxes and returned home. But they had become so subservient and inured to misery that they had submitted without a struggle to the continuance of their appalling slavery under Herod's successor ... He, as though anxious to prove himself the true son of his father, inaugurated his reign by putting 3,000 citizens to death ... they begged the Romans to pity the remnant of the Jews, and not to throw what was left of them to the savage beasts who would tear them to pieces, but unite their country with Syria and administer it through their own officials. This would show that men now falsely accused of sedition and aggression knew how to submit to reasonable authority.' (*The Jewish War.*)

But Augustus was an emperor in the Roman tradition. He could not agree to taking away the rights of the legitimate heirs of a dynasty installed by Rome herself. The Herodians ought to succeed the man who had been the best servant of Roman strength in Asia. How could men eager for freedom prefer direct foreign power—in this case Roman—to rule by Herod's children? Augustus knew perfectly well that Herod was not loved by his children, but had not Herod, of his own accord, lavished on Israel a mysterious Temple which crystallized in itself the relationship of the people to this obscure divinity worshipped by the Jews, which Pompey had been unable to describe in a way intelligible to a Roman? There was no question of hesitating. Augustus confirmed Herod's will. Archelaus was called ethnarch and received Judaea, Samaria and Idumaea. Thus, he did not reign over Herod's entire empire, but had Jerusalem and its Temple under his jurisdiction. Antipas received Galilee, Philip Bathanaea (all the land east of the Sea of Galilee), and Salome received the

town of Yabne, not far from the Mediterranean, as well as a palace at
Askalon.

*   *   *

The division of Herod's empire into four independent regions facilitated
the subversive work of the Zealots, but Augustus could not foresee this,
any more than he could the fact that the Zealots were gaining strength.
Their success with the people was becoming more and more imposing. The
people had not forgotten that Archelaus had had three thousand Jews put
to death in the Temple. They also realized that Augustus had hesitated
about making Archelaus Herod's successor. Archelaus was ethnarch—
not king. He was chosen to reign over the people, not to direct the state.
Finally, the man chosen by Rome did not have the political judgement
and authority of his father. He was hesitant, and lacked confidence.

The Zealot movement was born and spread rapidly through the
whole of Judaea. In view of the fact that they had to resort to brutal
methods to make up for their logistic inferiority, they were not immediately
recognized as the true defenders of the Jewish nation. They were forced
to go to ground in the countryside, to cut off roads, pillage caravans,
murder collaborators and Roman officials responsible for keeping order.
They were therefore, in the eyes of moderate Jews, or those favouring a
compromise with the occupiers, brigands and thieves.

A man called Simon, a former slave of Herod, got together a large
force, captured the town of Jericho, and burned down the palace. Armed
resistance groups took the east bank of the Jordan. Finally Athrongaeus,
along with his four powerful brothers, brought a state of insecurity to the
whole of Judaea. They attacked convoys of Roman army supply stores,
Jewish collaborators, and even those who had not made up their minds.

All this time Sabinus and the Roman legions were still besieged in
Jerusalem. Varus decided to leave Syria so as to come and help his
fellow countrymen. He mobilized four companies of cavalry and entered
Judaea, where he was joined by a great many Arab troops under the
command of King Aretas. The Arabs took Sempho, which they pillaged and burned. They spared nothing in their path and put the region
to sword and fire. The Romans devastated Emmaus, which its inhabitants
had abandoned, rightly fearing Roman reprisals after Anthrogaeus'
attacks against the Romans in the vicinity of the town.

The Jerusalem Jews, hearing of the formidable strength of Varus' army, lifted the siege and scattered over the countryside. Then a man-hunt began. The Romans combed the area around Jerusalem, seeking information about the revolutionaries, taking a great many prisoners and crucifying two thousand Jews. There was a band of ten thousand men who chose to surrender to Varus.

But the revolutionary feeling had taken hold of the whole country-side. Bands of irregular troops were constantly on the move and made a point of showing themselves to the people. The Zealots grew in authority, if not in power.

Spiritually, the Zealots were Pharisees. They believed that the soul was immortal, and that it would be judged in another world, where it could stay for ever, or—if it were not pure—returned to earth. They respected old men and never contradicted them. They believed that every-thing was in the hands of God but that man might, through his merits, modify the course of events and obtain Divine grace. Obviously in this respect the people's sympathies lay with the Pharisees and not the Sad-ducees whose legalism and intransigence isolated them from the mass of the people who loved to dream and hope for an improvement of their lot.

Politically, however, the Zealots were at variance with the Pharisees, because the former stressed the fact that the only master of the universe was God, and that no man might be called master. The Zealots 'agree in all other things with the Pharisaic notions; but they have an inviolable attachment to liberty; and they say that God is to be their only Ruler and Lord. They also do not value dying any kinds of death, nor indeed do they heed the death of their relations and friends, nor can any such fear make them call any man Lord. . . .' (*The Jewish Antiquities*). This apparently theocratic conception of society was nevertheless in accord with the idea that the liberty of the people was primordial. The most important and urgent principle of Zealot doctrine was therefore the freeing of the people from temporal domination. The aim of this liberation was evidently to bring the Jews under God's empire. Their doctrine was one of 'God and no other master,' but their denial of any authority and their method of fighting was influenced by strong libertarian concepts and revo-lutionary zeal. Despite the fact that the Sanhedrin was the highest and most authentic authority in traditional Jewish society, their scorn of the Sanhedrin and their indifference to it demonstrated their doctrinal radical-ism. Also, rather than invest Divine authority in priests who were con-sidered intermediaries through whom the will of God was expressed, the

Zealots preferred to preach Messianic optimism: they believed a day would come when God's envoy would lower all the barriers between men.

*   *   *

Archelaus was unable to impose his authority during the nine years that he ruled. Ambassadors once more took the road for Rome. Once more they brought to Augustus their grievances against Herod's son. Faced with such insistence, and understanding that the acquisition of Archelaus' possessions would be a welcome gift to the Empire, Augustus finally agreed to the demand of the ethnarch's subjects. The emperor summoned Archelaus to Rome and told him of his disgrace. Archelaus was to be exiled to Vienne in Gaul. Judaea, Samaria and Idumaea were annexed to the province of Syria and would therefore be directly under Roman administration. Coponius, a Roman member of the equestrian order, would have especial responsibility for the affairs of Judaea and the former provinces over which Herod's son had wielded authority. He would have the rank of procurator.

*   *   *

Satisfaction with Augustus' decision did not last long among the Jews. Once he was installed in Caesarea, Coponius' first action was to organize a census of the Jews, so that he could apply the imperial tax system more efficiently. The Jews opposed this not only because it meant an increase in the amount of taxes they would have to pay, but because Jewish society had always considered the counting of heads a fatal thing. A thousand years earlier, King David had ordered a census of the population of Israel, and when he heard the results had said: 'I have sinned greatly in that I have done: and now, I beseech thee, O Lord, take away the iniquity of thy servants; for I have done very foolishly.' (*I Samuel* XXIV, 10.) God punished Israel, and plague struck the people.

After that, the Jews never counted themselves, but arranged the number of beasts offered in sacrifice so as to obtain indirectly the number of people. Naturally the Zealots opposed the census imposed by Rome not only on religious or economic grounds, but because Roman control over the people would be greater and make peace-keeping operations easier. But the clergy—in the person of the High Priest Joazar, of the family of Beothos—gave its guarantee to the Roman project, so that the revolt that the Zealots wanted did not break out on this occasion. This did not prevent Coponius dismissing Joazar, once the census was over, and replacing him with Hanan Ananus as High Priest.

The new High Priest of the Jews heard of the death of Augustus with a feeling of anxiety. The year 14 began and the emperor had reigned for forty-four years. What Hanan knew of the reign of the first Roman emperor did not encourage him to optimism. Politically Augustus had not treated the Jews too badly. But he had made himself a high priest, had given new vigour to old pagan cults, such as that of the God Apollo. Would there not be an outburst of religious fanaticism now that Augustus was gone? Hanan soon heard that the Senate had just ordered the apotheosis of Augustus. His body had been burned on the Campus Martius, he had entered the ranks of the gods, and he was to have his own cult with priests and temples. Were the Romans going to abandon their liberalism in regard to religious matters, or would they seriously try to force the cult of idols on everyone?

Meanwhile in Judaea the burden of the taxes had fallen on the people. In less than ten years three Roman procurators had ruined the Jews. These representatives of imperial order each stayed in Judaea three years and had only one ambition, to get rich. They succeeded in so doing.

Tiberius, Augustus' adopted child—who was fifty-six years old—was chosen as successor. Rumours were already spreading through Jerusalem. Little was known about the emperor. Tiberius, they said, did not want public homage, had refused to let himself be called lord, would not have a temple built in his honour. Did this signify the awakening? Tiberius realized that as far as the complex affairs of Judaea were concerned, a rapid succession of procurators would provoke greater unrest. Newly arrived procurators, wanting to enrich themselves quickly, increased the fiscal burden and were only satiated after some years. Only then would they try to administer their territories objectively, considering the interests of the people. In the twenty-two years of Tiberius' reign, he sent only two procurators to Judaea—Gratus and Pilate. Tiberius loved to tell the following story: 'A great number of flies came about the sore places of a man that had been wounded, upon which, one of the standers-by pitied the man's misfortune, and thinking he was not able to drive away those flies himself, was going to drive them away for him; but he prayed him to let them alone; the other, by way of reply, asked him the reason of such a preposterous proceeding, in preventing relief from his present misery; to which he answered, "If thou drivest these flies away, thou wilt hurt me worse; for as these are already full of my blood, they do not crowd about me, nor pain me so much as before, but are sometimes more remiss, while the fresh ones that come, almost famished, and find me quite tired down already, will be my destruction."' (*The Jewish Antiquities.*)

In the face of such meekness—which was totally relative as far as the people were concerned—Philip, who had reigned over Galilee since Herod's death, decided to build the town of Tiberias by the lake of Kinereth in honour of Tiberius, for whom no act of praise was great enough. But the people did not see it that way. To call Jewish towns after deified emperors was sacrilege.

Pontius Pilate committed equally sacrilegious errors. He sent legions to Jerusalem bearing standards with the effigy of the emperor, which the Jews considered idols. An enormous crowd went, unarmed, to Caesarea and insulted the Roman envoy. Pilate's revenge was to have the seditious people beaten. Pilate probably realized that in spite of the burden of Roman occupation, the Jews would not submit, and would have no hesitation in showing their disapproval whenever their religious laws were violated, whatever the risks might be; so as a precaution he withdrew his troops from Jerusalem.

In the streets of Jerusalem the people were asking themselves what would be the spark that would ignite the revolt. The procurator's spies were quite certain that the Jews wanted to fight. They only needed an excuse. Pilate, a skilled politician, was not in the habit of taking unnecessary risks or of compromizing himself lightly. When Tiberius was murdered in 37, Pilate could flatter himself that after ten years as pro-consul he had not had any serious incursions in his career as a procurator. Nevertheless his name would go down in history.

*   *   *

In Rome Caius Caligula, Emperor of Rome by the grace of the gods and his uncle Tiberius, who had just died, was accustomed to hearing each morning the news of the vast empire over which he reigned. While eating breakfast he listened rather abstractedly to his minister unfold one by one the items in this daily bulletin of banalities. All was well in Rome, all was well in Greece, Asia, Africa, Gaul and Germany. Italy was calm and happy. So much for the serious matters. Next came the requests of the widows of former soldiers, petitions from ambitious officers, reports from spies obsessed by plots. The morning was too pleasant, the night had been too sweet. Nothing justified political worries so early. Like some god,

Caligula was happy to reign from his throne on high. *De minimis non curat praetor*! (The praetor does not concern himself with paltry matters.) But the voice of the minister became louder, more insistent. Caligula heard him mention the phrase 'rejection of the imperial cult.' The emperor asked his minister to repeat what he had said: 'The Greek inhabitants of Alexandria, who have been in the city since its foundation and are extremely careful about the cult of the emperor, accuse other citizens of Alexandria of not submitting to their religious obligations in respect to Caligula and of affirming loudly that they have no other gods except the one who is invisible.'

The minister, terrified by the reaction he had foreseen, drew back four paces. How could they refuse to worship him? It was not possible. Who were these people? Jews? He remembered that this was the same nationality as his friend Agrippa, who at present reigned over Galilee.

Caligula ordered a hearing of envoys from both sides on the reason for their quarrel, and the confrontation took place some days later. Apion spoke for the Greeks and in the name of the religious virtue of his fellow citizens. He was a grammarian and historian by profession, talkative and emphatic. His brief was simple, demagoguery was easy. He pointed out that in the Roman Empire there were many temples where the cult of the emperor was celebrated. Only the Jews refused to give religious honours to Caligula throughout Judaea and also in the foreign cities where they had acquired the right of citizenship. Philo was an intellectual, and a pure product of Alexandrian Judaism. He was a living synthesis of Graeco-Hebraic culture. He attempted to reply, but Caligula was beyond himself and drove the Jews out.

As he left the imperial palace, Philo reassured his friends. 'We must now hope more than ever. Since the emperor is so irritated by us, God would not fail to be favourable to us.'

Caligula was on the edge of a nervous crisis. He was obsessed by this refusal to worship him. He called one of his best officers, Patronius, and ordered him to go to Judaea, take up the governorship of the province and have a statue of Caligula set up in the Temple at Jerusalem. He ordered him to break Jewish pride and if necessary start a war. The announcement of this decision caused consternation among the Jews. Why could the emperor not be content with reigning over Judaea? Why did he have to be known as a god? Why did he have this pretension that Augustus never had? The Jews therefore sent representatives to Petronius, who was at Ptolemais. When he had heard what the Jews had to say, Petronius replied: 'Quite so but I too am bound to keep the law of my sovereign lord: If I break it and spare you I shall perish as I deserve. It will be the Emperor himself who will make war on you, not I. I am subject to authority just as you are.' (*The Jewish War*.)

The Jews replied: 'Since, therefore, thou art so disposed, O Petronius! that thou wilt not disobey Caius's epistles, neither will we transgress the commands of our law; and as we depend upon the excellency of our laws, and, by the labours of our ancestors, have continued hitherto, without suffering them to be transgressed, we dare not by any means suffer ourselves to be so timorous as to transgress those laws out of the fear of death, which God hath determined are for our advantage; and, if we fall into misfortunes we will bear them, in order to preserve our laws, as knowing that those who expose themselves to dangers, have good hope of escaping them: because God will stand on our side when, out of regard to him, we undergo afflictions, and sustain the uncertain turns of fortune. But if we should submit to thee, we should be greatly reproached for our cowardice, as thereby showing ourselves ready to transgress our law; and we should incur the great anger of God also, who, even thyself being judge, is superior to Caius.' (*The Jewish Antiquities*.)

The ambassador's arguments were not only founded on ancient Jewish tradition, but also on the recent doctrine of the Zealots. God's primacy over Caligula was ironically underlined and the acceptance of the consequences of the Jewish refusal was clearly shown. When Petronius had thought for a while he called together a large number of the Jews and said to them: 'I do not think it just to have such a regard to my own safety and honour as to refuse to sacrifice them for your preservation, who are so many in number, and endeavour to preserve the regard that is due to your law; which, as it hath come down to you from your forefathers, so do you esteem it worthy of your utmost contention to preserve it: nor, with the supreme assistance and power of God, will I be so hardy as to suffer your temple to fall into contempt by the means of the imperial authority. I will, therefore, send to Caius, and let him know what your resolutions are, and will assist your suit as far as I am able, that you may not be exposed to suffer on account of the honest designs you have proposed to yourselves; and may God be your assistant, for his authority is beyond all the contrivances and power of men; and may he procure you the preservation of your ancient laws, and may not he be deprived, though without your consent, of his accustomed honours.' (*The Jewish Antiquities*.)

The Jews had every reason to think that God had come to their aid. Petronius' message to Caligula did not arrive in Rome until after the death of the mad emperor. Petronius realized that the God of the Jews did not abandon those who believed in Him. Caligula was assassinated as he left a theatre. Everyone who had endured the madman's bloody oppression was overjoyed at the news.

*   *   *

Agrippa I was happy to have succeeded his grandfather, Herod the Great, as King of Galilee, although the inheritance had diminished in size. Nevertheless he was bored, and missed Rome. As did others before him, he bided his time and travelled, amusing himself and making plans for the future. Agrippa often thought about his happy youth in Rome. When he was six years old he had been sent there by his father and had known Claudius and Caligula. He had openly wished for Tiberius' death in front of Caligula, but also in the presence of a slave, who then denounced him. He was imprisoned for six months, but set free by Caligula. Since then he had reigned over part of Herod's former empire.

On New Year's Day 41, Agrippa I was visiting Rome. When the theatres ended, the streets of Rome were full of people being pursued by the emperor's personal guard. In the grip of a kind of bloody madness, the guards were killing everyone in their path. Caligula had just been murdered. The succession was wide open. Agrippa hurried to Claudius' house. They had been children, then adolescents, together at the court of Rome. He advised Claudius to accept the succession. The army wanted him. Claudius let himself be moved and took possession of the throne. One of his first decisions was to enlarge Agrippa's territory, giving him the missing provinces and above all Jerusalem. Agrippa was to be the only successor of Herod the Great to reign over the whole of Judaea.

The Jews did not complain about this choice. They knew that Agrippa was the grandson of Mariamne, of the Hasmonaean dynasty, the only legitimate dynasty in the Jews' eyes. Agrippa respected and broadly practised the Jewish religion. He wanted peace and tried to establish friendly relations with Judaea's neighbours. Relations with Rome were excellent, and Claudius allowed the Jews living in Alexandria or Rome the right to practise their religion without imposing other gods on them. In the Temple Agrippa offered sacrifices of thanksgiving. He appointed a new high priest and remitted taxes due on each house in Jerusalem.

Furthermore, since Agrippa came to the throne, the regime of the procurators had been abolished. In spite of their intransigence and the certainty that there should be no more kings to reign over Israel, the Jews
accepted with relief the departure of the Roman procurator and the rule of
a prince. He was latinized, but at least he had the happiness of the people
at heart. During this period the Zealots were fairly quiet. Anarchy reigned
outside the towns, but there did not appear to be any positive affront to
the authority of Agrippa the Great.

At sunset on a day in July 44, the inhabitants of Jerusalem felt the
arrival of the cool of the evening that they had so long waited for. The
last worshippers came down from the Temple where the afternoon sacrifices had been celebrated in a suffocating atmosphere. Soon the heavy
sanctuary doors would be closed and Jerusalem would live its less chaste
night life. The first fires in the Roman camp were lit as if to take over
from those in the Temple which had just gone out, except for the perpetual
flame which was jealously watched by the priests. But in the northern
part of Jerusalem a noise began, and the excitement gradually reached
all parts of the Holy City. A rumour was circulating that Agrippa had
been assassinated at Caesarea. The news was soon confirmed and the
Roman legions were put on the alert. Everyone wondered who had killed
the Jewish king. Surely not the Zealots. Nor the Pharisees or the Sadducees, for Agrippa consulted them regularly and involved them in public
affairs, Surely not the Roman soldiers, for the Emperor Claudius was a
childhood friend of Agrippa. So who could it be. It was obvious to everyone that the crime was the work of the Greeks of Caesarea, who were
jealous of Agrippa's influence in Rome and his good neighbourly relations
with Egypt and Syria. They had poisoned him. Now that Agrippa was
dead, would there be a return to the much hated rule of the procurators?

In a Jerusalem house, a man named Tholomaeus was wondering
whether a return to direct administration from Rome would not facilitate
the revolutionary designs of the Zealots. Since his childhood he had lived
in the countryside as a brigand, but gradually, through violent skirmishes
with the imperial legions, he had been able to assert himself and become
leader of a strongly organized band of Zealots. The arrival of a new
procurator to govern Judaea in place of Agrippa would certainly favour
his plan and rouse the people from their lethargy. Tholomaeus knew that

the dead king had a son of seventeen who lived in Rome. Both Agrippa II and his sister, the famous Berenice, were being brought up in Rome.

Tholomaeus quickly collected some provisions in a bag, slid his dagger into his belt, threw an immense cloak round his shoulders and hurried off into the night to join his men. He knew that the moment of action was very near.

In Rome Emperor Claudius was very upset by Agrippa's death. His first reaction was to send the dead king's son to Judaea immediately, but he knew that the young man would not carry much weight as ruler of the kingdom of Judaea. There had to be a return to the rule of the procurators. Claudius appointed Cupius Fadus, a member of the equestrian order. Cupius was a cynical man, full of the bitterness that derives from excessive ambition and a thwarted career.

Fadus set himself two goals: extinction of the centres of revolutionary agitation and destruction of the latent resistance of the religious party. The new procurator was well briefed by the spies in his pay and wasted no time in capturing Tholomaeus, who ended his career as leader of the Zealots with his arms spread out on a cross, in a burning hot part of the mountains of Judaea, his last look directed towards the redeeming Temple.

Fadus did not stop there. He summoned the people responsible for the sacrifice and the representatives of the inhabitants of Jerusalem, and ordered them to take to the Antonia fortress the High Priest's vestments which were only to be used on the Day of Atonement. If the Jews wanted to honour their God according to the rules for the Day of Atonement, they would have to be peaceful during the whole year.

When the news of Fadus' decision reached Rome, Claudius decided to recall the over-ambitious official. He took advantage of the occasion to state the imperial policy of the Jewish question.

'Claudius Caesar Germanicus, tribune of the people the fifth time, and designed consul the fourth time, and imperator the tenth time, the father of his country, to the magistrates, senate, and people, and the whole nation of the Jews, sendeth greeting. Upon the representation of your ambassadors to me by Agrippa my friend, whom I have brought up, and have now with me, and who is a person of very great piety, who are come to give me thanks for the care I have taken of your nation, and to entreat me, in an earnest and obliging manner, that they may have the holy vestments, with the crown belonging to them, under their power—I grant their request, as that excellent person

Vitellius, who is very dear to me, had done before me. And I have complied with your desire, in the first place, out of regard to that piety which I profess, and because I would have every one worship God according to the laws of their own country; And this I do also, because I shall hereby gratify king Herod and the young Agrippa, whose sacred regards to me, and earnest good-will, I am well acquainted with, and with whom I have the greatest friendship, and whom I highly esteem, and look on as persons of the best character.' (*The Jewish Antiquities.*)

*   *   *

'Thou, O Lord, art mighty for ever . . . thou causest the wind to blow and the rain to fall.' Since their beginnings this agricultural people had raised this prayer to heaven; but for the last nine months, when this point was reached in the service, voices sounded anxious. Jerusalem was hungry. The wadis and wells were dry, the ground parched and the sun like lead above the Temple. There were no more animals offered in sacrifice and all the priests could bring to the altar from time to time was a thin dove whose blood did not even flow on to the sacred stone. In the streets dust was everywhere. The Jews were waiting for a cooling wind. They were unhappy and turned their anger against Rome. Why did their protectors not guarantee urgent restocking of supplies for the city?

The Zealots were going to attempt to put oil on the fire. In 46 the Zealot movement was exactly fifty years old. The results were not encouraging. All the leaders of the resistance had been executed, beginning with Judas the Galilean, the founder of the party. But his two older sons, Jacob and Simon, were still alive. They tried to decide on a strategy. There was certainly no question of a general uprising against Rome in a time of famine. The people were weak and would not be able to take on well-fed soldiers. But advantage had to be taken of the general dissatisfaction, and efforts at propaganda relaunched. Moreover, the Emperor Claudius maintained that he was the Jews' friend, and the people were credulous enough to attach importance to his protestations of friendship. Luckily for the Zealots it had just been learned that the new Roman procurator in Judaea was to be Tiberius Alexander, the son of an Alexandrian Jew famous for his great wealth. Tiberius Alexander had forsaken his father's faith for that of idolatrous Rome. For this reason it was a major political blunder to appoint such a man to such a post. The Zealots would take advantage of this and exploit the situation.

Jacob and Simon decided to increase their activities. They took all

the risks and led most of the actions personally. They knew that if something unfortunate had to happen to them, their young brother, who was
still a child, could one day take over and continue their father's tradition.
The boy on whom the hopes of the resistance rested was called Menahem.
For the time being his only activity was studying the Torah and the holy
books, but soon he would learn the use of arms. That morning, as he
waved good-bye to his brothers who were leaving on an operation, Menahem had no idea that he would never see them again.

Tiberius Alexander was not only one of the most notorious young
men of the city, an idle rich man greedy for power and honours. He was
also an experienced and clever soldier. As he watched the development
of an attack against a Roman camp in the vicinity of Jerusalem, he noticed
that the brigands who were giving the orders were isolated on a promontory. It took only a few fast, well-armed men to capture the two Jewish
leaders. They were brought in chains to the procurator's feet and then
crucified, while Tiberius celebrated with his officers. In their slow death
under a pitiless sun, their last view was of the Dead Sea, and in the far
distance they thought they could see the fortress of Masada guarding the
Jerusalem road in the south.

At the end of this day, everyone knew, across the whole of Judaea,
that the traitor had crucified the venerated leaders of the resistance, the
sons of Judas the Galilean. Claudius was informed immediately, and being aware of the danger of a major confrontation, recalled Tiberius
Alexander.

The emperor appointed a cruel member of the equestrian order to
Judaea, whose reputation for being firm was well earned. Physically and
morally Cumanus seemed to be the reincarnation of Tiberius Alexander.
The procession of procurators continued.

The next year, during Passover, a startling event took place near
the Temple. A Roman soldier 'pulled up his garment and bent over in-
decently, turning his backside towards the Jews and making a noise as
indecent as his attitude.' (*The Jewish War*.) Because of the people's
violent reaction, the procurator poured reinforcements into the Antonia
fortress, so as to be ready for any eventuality. But the Jews took fright,
and in the course of the panic that ensued twenty thousand Jews died of
suffocation. The people cried for vengeance. A Zealot called Eleazar who,
since the crucifixion of the older sons of the Galilean had been in command of the Zealots, came to the rescue and attacked the towns of
Samaria. A clash with the Roman troops would have been inevitable had

not certain Pharisees succeeded in persuading the people to go home and not persist in their behaviour. Cumanus was in fact marching on Jerusalem with cavalry, four cohorts, and a number of armed Samaritans. The skirmishes with the Zealots left many dead, but the battle of Jerusalem was avoided. When Cumanus arrived everything was quiet and the Jews were only busy at prayers and sacrifices to their God. The procurator thought that he would be able to triumph by having all the resistance fighters captured and crucified. Moreover he decided to exile the high priest to Rome. Once more the Jews decided to complain to the emperor. A new delegation went to Rome, where young Agrippa was still residing. He brought about Cumanus' disgrace. He was now twenty-six years old, and Claudius decided to make him take up his functions as King of Batanaea and ethnarch. In this second capacity he ruled over the entire Jewish nation. The Roman procurator had the upper hand in Judaea and Samaria including, naturally, Jerusalem. But as a special privilege, Agrippa II administered the Temple and had the power to appoint the high priest. There was no fear of conflict over spheres of duty. Agrippa II would follow Rome in everything, since he knew both its power and its kindness.

*　　*　　*

In Upper Galilee, some distance from the town of Sepphoris, shadowy forms moved around in the calm, starry night. They moved slowly, bumping into one another, climbing in silence towards the cavern pointed out to them. Eleazar had called together the leaders of the resistance. He wanted to examine the new situation created by the enthronement of Agrippa II. Eleazar got up and his shadow, projected on the back wall of the cave, made him seem immense. He checked to make sure that everyone was there, and then reminded them of the ultimate objective of the Zealots: total independence. The immediate aim was to train the entire nation in the struggle against Rome. As long as the incidents were confined to the countryside, which was more or less desert, Zealot influence over the people would obviously remain limited. As it happened the Zealots had no choice. The Romans had brought off several very rewarding punitive actions. The legions were beginning to organize themselves for restricted battles, in open order. The Zealots were sustaining considerable losses. There was only one solution. They would have to mingle with the urban population and strike at Roman leaders and Jewish collaborators.

So the first Jewish terrorist movement—the *sicarii*—was born in the history of Israel. Their method was simple. They mingled with the crowd, in broad daylight in Jerusalem or even in the Temple precincts. They were dressed in full cloaks with several folds. They could therefore easily hide short daggers and they operated in the Holy City. They never struck blindly when they planned to assault Jews, but they readily attacked isolated Roman officers. The Temple guards could never search them adequately. Their weapons were so small and their cloaks so vast. When they had identified their victim they approached and took advantage of the movement of the crowd, the call of a tradesman or the shout of a child, to strike the blow. They then mixed with the people shouting 'Murder,' consequently increasing the confusion, and eventually were able to escape.

The High Priest Jonathan was killed in this way. The high priests collaborated with Rome and the people did not like them. They represented the party who stood for capitulation. They approved the Roman census, and were agents of the Roman tax system, when they should have been driven to revolt by the holiness of their office. Several decades later the Talmud recorded the expression of popular hatred for the high-priestly dynasties: 'What a disaster the family of Beothos, woe to their lances. What a disaster the family of Hanan, woe to their hissing of vipers. ... They are high priests themselves, their sons are treasurers, their sons-in-law officers and their servants strike the people with their sticks.' (*Talmud*, Passachim 57a.)

The aim of the *sicarii* was to make the people realize the necessity for revolt. Any method was to be allowed. They therefore had no hesitation in acting while the pilgrimage feasts were in progress, when a vast crowd usually came to Jerusalem. But did they manage to create the climate of insecurity suitable for the achievement of their undertaking? Josephus, who was by nature favourable to the established order and who later became a Roman agent, was concerned for his own safety and described the atmosphere in Jerusalem in this way: 'More terrible than the crimes themselves was the fear they aroused, every man as in war hourly expecting death. They watched at a distance for their enemies, and not even when their friends came near did they trust them: yet in spite of their suspicions and precautions they were done to death; such was the suddenness of the conspirators' attack and their skill in avoiding detection.' (*The Jewish War*.)

The *sicarii* extended their actions from Jerusalem to the large centres of Galilee where there were many mountainous hideouts. In fact many of them originally came from this part of the country, which was full of proselytes. Since they had recently accepted the Jewish faith, they were fired with aggressive zeal.

*   *   *

Subversive activity spread throughout Judaea as a whole, due as much to the activity of the *sicarii* as the general feeling that the Messiah was soon to appear. The theory of the Zealots spread in the Temple, the schools, even the streets. Everyone began to believe that liberation would come through a man sent by God, a Messiah. Of course this hope had always been fundamental for the Jews, but now the Zealots maintained that the Anointed, the Son of David, could only come if the people began their armed struggle against the Romans first. God's envoy would head the Jewish revolt and lead to victory those who believed in him. This explains both the large numbers of enchanters, magicians and false messiahs of every sort in the years around 50, and also the fear the Roman administration had for such movements, which it had no hesitation in opposing with force. In fact all the Messianic movements of the time were revolutionary movements.

The procurator felt that danger was imminent. He led the fight against this kind of collective madness. He heard that an enchanter had arrived from Egypt and had succeeded in gathering thirty thousand men whom he had persuaded to follow him into the desert. The Egyptian followed inspiration rather than considerations of security. The desert was not at all a safe place. The Romans could more easily spot and cut down a band of that size in the desert than in the mountains of Judaea or Galilee. But the enchanter allowed himself to become a victim of the prophetic theme of the desert. There had never risen up a prophet in Israel who had not gone through a stage of purification with his followers in the desert. The Essenes regarded it as a rule of their community 'to separate oneself from the dwelling of the men of evil' and to 'seek the desert to prepare there the way of the Lord.' (*Dead Sea Scrolls.*)

Moreover, the prophets seemed to have a special liking for the Mount of Olives, from where one overlooked the Temple and the whole city. The Egyptian was consistent in this detail also, and gathered several hundred followers on the Mount of Olives, where he announced that the Temple would be destroyed and that everyone would be able to enter the holy place without going through doors. This was the third theme common to all the 'magicians' of the time, the destruction of the Temple. But the motivating force of these great gatherings around a magician was the fight against the Romans whose defeat and departure from Judaea were announced. Finally, one point common to all these movements was the disappearance of the agitator after his defeat.

All the Messianic movements seemed to follow these main principles. The Egyptian who flourished as a prophet at the time was no exception. He was beaten and disappeared without trace. But the memory of him was so firmly fixed in people's minds that much later his followers asked Paul of Tarsus, the future St Paul, if he was the Egyptian.

But this was not the first time that a procurator had had to fight against this kind of prophetically motivated revolt. For the last twenty years or so they had followed one another virtually without let up. The most famous of the Messianic movements of the 1st century had arisen during the rule of Pontius Pilate, in about the year 30.

*   *   *

Who was Jesus of Nazareth? Romans, Pharisees, Sudduceean priests, his own disciples, spies, unknown people all asked Jesus to reveal his true identity. His replies were never clear. But over the course of the long months of his preachings, they all sensed his growing conviction that he was to herald the Messiah waited for by Israel: then that he was the Messiah himself, and finally that he was the Son of God. But Jesus could not disclose his plans. His enemies were too powerful. He could easily have had himself recognized as the Messiah of Israel through his talents as a miraculous healer, and his great knowledge of the Jewish Law, but to do so would be tantamount to admitting that he was leader of a revolutionary movement whose aim was to drive the Romans out of Judaea. Therefore it was necessary to be prudent.

When Peter recognized Jesus as the Messiah, he was told emphatically not to talk about it to anyone (*Mark* VIII, 30). When the High Priest asked him whether he was the Messiah, Jesus replied: 'Hereafter shall the Son of Man sit on the right hand of the power of God.' (*Luke* XXII, 69.) This was an avowal of the fact that he was the Messiah, but it was only comprehensible to the High Priest himself and to the Jewish scholars who knew Psalm 110, in which God asks His Messiah to sit at His right hand. But the Romans could not understand such cryptic language and did not appreciate the reference. When Pontius Pilate asked him, 'Art thou the King of the Jews?' Jesus replied, 'Thou sayest' which could either mean 'You say so; you have no proof; it is inexact,' or 'You say so; you have told the truth; it is as you say.' But there is no doubt of the fact that Jesus was crucified both as King of the Jews, as Messiah, and as leader of a revolutionary movement. The inscription on the Cross—King of the Jews—testifies to the fact, as well as Roman law which said: 'Instigators of revolt or rebellion are, according to their status, liable to be crucified, thrown to wild beasts, or deported to an island.'

Jesus' attitude to the Pharisees was indicative of the revolutionary nature of his activity. The Scribes and Pharisees were always called hypocrites by Jesus, who held that they did not match their words with their deeds. Everyone knew perfectly well that the Zealots agreed with the Pharisees in everything except the acceptance of a master other than God. Jesus taught: 'The scribes and the Pharisees sit in Moses' seat: All therefore whatsoever they bid you observe, that observe and do; but do not ye after their works: for they say, and do not.' (*Matthew*, XXIII, 2, 3.) Did Jesus not mean that the Pharisees were right, but that they would not do their duty and revolt?

John the Baptist, inspired by a profound belief in the necessity for the purification of the Jews, baptized Jesus, as he baptized all who came to him in a spirit of true repentance. He heard that Jesus worked miracles, and that the people of Galilee saw in him the Messiah. The Baptist was gratified by this news, because he began to think that he was himself Elijah, the last prophet, and the man who announced the imminent appearance of the Messiah. John the Baptist sent men to Jesus to ask him whether he was the Messiah or not. Jesus based his reply on a prophecy of Isaiah (XXXV, 5-6): 'Go and shew John again those things which ye do see and hear. The blind receive their sight, and the lame walk, the lepers are cleansed and the deaf hear, the dead are raised up, and the poor have the gospel preached to them. And blessed is he, whosoever shall not be offended in me.' (*Matthew* II, 4-6). Jesus answered John by pointing to what he was doing. He did not say that he was the Messiah. But he did tell his disciples that John the Baptist was Elijah: '. . . this is that Elijah, which was for to come. He that hath ears to hear, let him hear.' (*Matthew* XI, 14, 15.) So the people became more and more convinced that the time was near and that John the Baptist was Elijah. When Herod Antipas —who reigned over Galilee—had John beheaded, the people would not believe that he was dead. Many thought that Jesus was John. Antipas shared this belief and wanted to put Jesus to death also. The reasons for

John's execution were evidently political. Antipas reproached him for having encouraged agitation in the desert and prepared an armed uprising against authority. Throughout Judaea everyone was talking about the adventure of John the Baptist and the reasons for his arrest:

'He was a good man who exhorted the Jews to exercise virtue, both as to righteousness towards one another, and piety towards God, and so to come to baptism; for that the washing with water would be acceptable to him, if they made use of it, not in order to the putting away, or the remission of some sins only, but for the purification of the body: supposing still that the soul was thoroughly purified beforehand by righteousness. Now when many others came to crowd about him, for they were greatly moved or pleased by hearing his words, Herod feared lest the great influence John had over the people might put it into his power and inclination to raise a rebellion, for they seemed ready to do anything he should advise, thought it best, by putting him to death, to prevent any mischief he might cause, and not bring himself into difficulties, by sparing a man who might make him repent of it when it should be too late. Accordingly he was sent a prisoner, out of Herod's suspicious temper, to Macheras, the castle I before mentioned, and was there put to death.' (*The Jewish Antiquities*.)

According to some people, Jesus was leader of a band of nine hundred rebels. According to others—equally anti-Christian—Jesus assembled ten thousand men on the Mount of Olives. When Jesus was arrested a disciple asked him, 'Lord, shall we smite with the sword?' (Luke XXII, 49.) But 'one of them which were with Jesus stretched out his hand, and drew his sword, and struck a servant of the high priest's, and smote off his ear. Then said Jesus unto him, "Put up again thy sword into his place: for all they that take the sword shall perish with the sword." ' (*Matthew* XXVI, 51, 52.)

On several occasions Jesus seemed to want to drag his disciples into revolt. 'But now, he that hath a purse, let him take it, and likewise his scrip: and he that hath no sword, let him sell his garment, and buy one.' (*Luke* XXII, 36.) 'Think not that I am come to send peace on earth: I come not to send peace, but a sword.' (*Matthew* X, 34.)

Moreover, Jesus' immediate disciples, otherwise known as the apostles, did not seem particularly suitable men to spread his spiritual message. They were more like lieutenants in an armed band. One of them, Simon, was known as a Zealot, and Simon Peter was called Bar Jonah, which does not mean son of Jonah, but member of the resistance. *Baryon* in Aramaic means a man who lives in the open air—because he has a fear of living in town. Jesus was a war leader.

But some Jews were quite right in believing that the Kingdom of God, to which both Jesus and the Zealots referred, would only be achieved by putting an end to sin, and not through force of arms. Observance of the Law of Moses would entail *ipso facto* the departure of the Romans. Jewish tradition stated: 'If Israel is ready to observe the commandments of the Law which was given to it, no people, no empire will reign over it. For what does the Law say? Take upon you the yoke of my name, vie one with another in the fear of God and have charity one towards another.' (Commentary on *Deuteronomy* 32, 29.)

Be that as it may, it is certain that Jesus—even if he finally threw off his doubts about whether or not he was the Messiah—was forced to make a speech alluding to the matter so as to be recognized as God's envoy. His very teaching had to be given in the form of parables because any clear expression might entail the same fate as John the Baptist had suffered. He would appear to be the founder of a sect which would, in the political context of the age, make him a revolutionary. Nevertheless Jesus took risks, otherwise his teaching would have remained cryptic and would have attracted no one. He spoke clearly on the moral plane. He taught the traditional teaching of Hillel, giving pride of place to love of one's neighbour as the means of salvation. In preaching love, Jesus hoped that he would not be accused of preaching war. But the Romans did not attach importance to the content of his teaching: what concerned them above all was that large mystical gatherings should not disrupt public order. Jesus was aware of this danger, which is why he was generally followed only by a small number of desciples. He did not want to find himself in the same situation as the Essenes, who, retaining an original teaching, had to isolate themselves from the world and live in communities in the desert separated from the rest of the people. Jesus knew that he lived in a revolutionary climate and that all the acts of the Jews had a political dimension. In spite of everything he chose to give his teaching— which many considered as a new Jewish sensitivity—wide diffusion by refusing any rupture with the modern world. The parabolic aspect that he sometimes gave his teaching was a very thin disguise. His disciples and friends were not unaware of the fact that he held the key to certain know- ledge. In spite of the ultimate message of his teaching which was love and peace, Jesus played a revolutionary role in the Judaea of the time, in the sense that he finally let himself be acknowledged as the Messiah. God's envoy was, in the eyes of the people, a liberator whose mission was to drive out the Romans. In this respect Jesus' attitude was different, when faced with the same problem, from that of the Essenes who had retreated into the desert.

*   *   *

The Essenes' withdrawal did not mean that they were indifferent to the Judaeo-Roman conflict. Because of their isolation the Romans were curious to know about the organization of this sect. By nationality the Essenes were Jews. They lived in very closed communities to which only men were admitted. They did not marry, maintaining that traffic with women weakened man's resolution. This did not prevent them from receiving children committed to their care, and from bringing them up as their own. The Essenes despised riches and pleasure. They bought nothing and sold nothing. The fruit of their labours was shared among all the members of the community. They had deep respect for their superiors and never became angry. They scrupulously observed the Divine requirements relating to the Sabbath, and would suffer death rather than violate them. They believed in the beyond and the immortality of the soul. In some Essene communities, where marriage was practised, the man would watch the woman he had chosen for a space of three years before contracting a union, to convince himself of her perfect health and ability to have children.

The Essenes numbered about four thousand in AD 30. They had renounced animal sacrifice, and because they were cut off from the Temple worship, it had little importance for them. In this way the Essenes had inaugurated the synagogical tradition of Judaism. They met in places of prayer and recited verses of the Torah, which the most learned among them then commented upon. Essene teaching was devoted entirely to morality. They avoided logic which they considered a verbal game devoid of interest, and physics to the extent that it related to a universe that was not man's. Finally, the Essenes were generally people of a mature age.

John the Essene, for example, knew the military rule which reveals the true character of the sect. This rule contains a group of instructions of a technical nature in respect of the war which the Sons of Light (the Essenes) will wage against the Sons of Darkness (the unbelievers). The hate that the Essenes had for their enemies was not to be the result of a spiritual experience—such as the hatred of evil or the Devil—but that of everyday life. There is no doubt but that their enemy was present in a terrifying way. Moreover, the Essenes considered themselves as soldiers. In the war manuscripts, the Sons of Darkness are called Kittim. This is evidently a code name chosen for security purposes. It can only mean the Romans. Therefore the war against the Kittim, for which the Essenes were preparing themselves, would be the one which the Jews would wage against Roman might. The Romans were the masters of the inhabited world, and their defeat would mean that the Sons of Light would reign over the whole universe. This would result in the ultimate victory of the forces of good.

Here is an extract from the War Rule, defined by the Essenes, as found among the *Dead Sea Scrolls*:

'. . . . The dominion of the Kittim shall come to an end and iniquity shall be vanquished, leaving no remnant; for the sons of darkness there shall be no escape. The seasons of righteousness shall shine over all the ends of the earth: they shall go on shining until all the seasons of darkness are consumed and, at the season appointed by God, His exalted greatness shall shine eternally to the peace, blessing, glory, joy, and long life of all the sons of light.

'On the day when the Kittim fall, there shall be battle and terrible carnage before the God of Israel, for that shall be the day appointed from ancient times for the battle of destruction of the sons of darkness. At that time, the assembly of gods and the hosts of men shall battle, causing great carnage; on the day of calamity, the sons of light shall battle with the company of darkness amid the shouts of a mighty multitude and the clamour of gods and men to make manifest the might of God. And it shall be a time of great tribulation for the people which God shall redeem; of all its afflictions none shall be as this, from its sudden beginning until its end of eternal redemption.

'On the day of their battle against the Kittim they shall set out for carnage. In three lots shall the sons of light brace themselves in battle to strike down iniquity, and in three lots shall Satan's host gird itself to thrust back the company of God. And when the hearts of the detachments of foot-soldiers faint, then shall the might of God fortify the heart of the sons of light. And with the seventh lot, the mighty hand of God shall bring down the army of Satan, and all the agents of his kingdom, and all the members of his company in everlasting destruction . . .'

It seems that in the spirit of the Essenes the fall of the Roman Empire would see the beginning of the universal reign of the Sons of

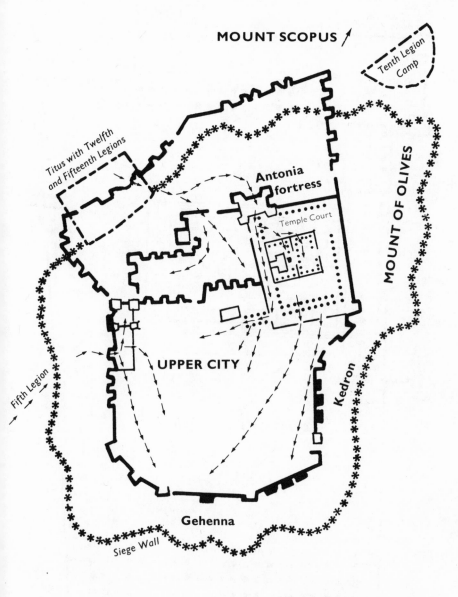

MOUNT SCOPUS

Tenth Legion
Camp

Titus with Twelfth
and Fifteenth Legions

Antonia
fortress

Temple Court

MOUNT OF OLIVES

UPPER CITY

Kedron

Fifth Legion

Gehenna

Siege Wall

Roman Legions →   →   →   →

A map of Jerusalem showing the Roman legions' attack in AD 70

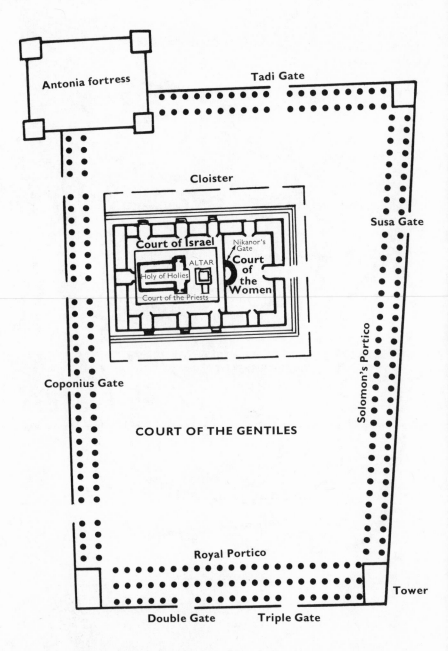

A diagram of the Temple which Herod the Great reconstructed
around the old sanctuary

A model of Herod's magnificent Palace in Jerusalem

A model of the city of Jerusalem before its destruction
by the Roman legions in AD 70

A bust of Vespasian's son, Titus

A panel from the Arch of Titus in Rome showing Titus's
triumphant return

Light. So there was apparently little doubt that the Essenes, hidden away in the desert, were preparing themselves for war with the Romans, just as the Zealots and the *sicarii* were laying ambushes for the Roman troops and executing collaborators in the streets of Jerusalem.

The Master of Justice was the leader of the Essene order. His real name was never mentioned, rather in the way that the Torah forbade God's real name to be spoken. This precaution apparently assured the safety of the Master. He was given a variety of names: the One Master, the Priest, the Seeker of the Law, the Star and the Legislator.

Whereupon the question once more arises, was the Master of Justice the Messiah? The Essenes paid particular attention to several Biblical prophets who were constantly studied by the sect. For them the Messiah had to fulfil three fundamental requirements: to be the Messiah of Israel, the chief lay person of the Jewish nation; the son of Aaron, in other words the Priest par excellence, the priestly Messiah, and finally the prophet of modern times—the man who, in his day, could tell the people the past significance and the present value of the promises made by God to Israel through the intermediary of the prophets in times past. The recapitulation of the prophecies as a whole and their interpretation in their modern context ought to facilitate a new definition of the conduct of Israel, whose ultimate goal was the victory of the Sons of Light over the Sons of Darkness.

There is no doubt that for the Essenes the Master fulfilled all three roles. In the field of prophecy, according to Essene writings, the Master is 'the man through whom God has founded doctrine and in whose heart he has placed intelligence so that he might open the source of knowledge for all the intelligent.' For the Essenes the Master was very like Moses, and moreover it was through him' that God 'would distinguish between the just and the guilty.' The Master ensured religious mediation between God and the people. Furthermore, the fact that the Essenes were preparing for battle against the Kittim, as well as the evidence provided by their War Rule, proves that the Master was the supreme fighter, the one who would unquestionably establish the reign of the Sons of Light.

Were the Essenes then a war party such as the Zealots were? It is probable that Menahem, son of Judas of Galilee, was the Master. His grandfather, father and two brothers had been killed by the Roman occupiers. In common with his father, Manahem—the unconquerable man of Israeli resistance—was a scholar, and fulfilled all the requirements of

purity required for the priesthood. Moreover he played a determining role
in the unleashing of the Judaeo-Roman war, to which he gave a truly
mystical dimension.

*   *   *

In 64, the year of the fire of Rome, Nero appointed a new procurator to
Judaea. His name was Gessius Florus.: 'Gessius boasted of the wrongs he
did to the nation and, as if sent as public executioner to punish condemned
criminals, indulged in every kind of robbery and violence. When pitiable
things happened, he showed himself the most heartless of men; when
disgraceful things, the most disgusting. No one ever had less use for truth
or thought out more subtle methods of crime. Making a profit out of
individuals he considered poor sport: he stripped whole cities, ruined
communities, and virtually announced to the entire country that everyone
might be a bandit if he chose, so long as he himself received a rake-off.'
(*The Jewish War.*)

In fact Florus wanted to drive the Jews to revolt because he thought
peace injurious for a procurator who wanted to get rich. In peacetime the
Jews could go to Rome and complain to the emperor. On one occasion,
maintaining that the Jews in Jerusalem had not given him all the honours
due to his rank, he unleashed his troops and 3,360 Jews died—many of
them Roman citizens. To increase their wrath Florus enticed the majority
of the Jews out of Jerusalem in an attempt to gain access to the Temple
and steal its treasure. The Jews hurriedly returned, destroyed the gallery
which connected the Antonia fortress to the Court of the Gentiles and
confronted Florus. After several furious attacks the procurator gave up
and returned to Caesarea. From there he sent a report to his superior,
the Governor of Syria, Cestius Gallus. He shamelessly claimed that the
Jews had revolted, and that war was inevitable. The Jews begged Agrippa
II to send an embassy to Rome to demand that Florus be recalled and
disciplined. An envoy from the Governor of Syria was well received, but
the people were anxious to rid themselves entirely of Rome's oppression.
A young captain of the Temple, Eleazar, son of the High Priest Ananias,
decided to join the ranks of the Zealots. As an initial act of revolt, he
stopped the twice-daily sacrifices which were made in the Temple in
honour of the emperor. In the religious context it was an overt declaration
of war. There was great excitement in the city and rumours were spread-

ing. Short-lived prophets went about the city announcing the imminent destruction of the Temple.

*   *   *

Faced with these troubles, Agrippa decided to act. He called together the Jewish leaders and the inhabitants of Jerusalem. He addressed them, in an attempt to disarm them, in a speech which is a piece of eloquence worthy of inclusion in the annals of treason:

'If I had found you all eager for war with the Romans, whereas in fact the most honest and sincere section of the people are bent on keeping the peace, I should not have come forward to address you or ventured to give you advice, for it is a waste of breath to say anything in favour of a wise course when the audience is unanimously in favour of a foolish one. But some of you are young men with no experience of the horrors of war, others are too sanguine about the prospects of independence, others are led on by selfish ambition and the profit to be made out of weaker men if the explosion occurs. So in the hope that these men may learn sense and change their ways, and that the folly of a few may not be visited on good citizens, I felt obliged to call you all together and tell you what I think is best . . .

'It would be absurd because of the trifling misdemeanours of one man to go to war with a whole nation, and such a nation—a nation that does not even know what it is all about! Our grievances can be quickly put right; the same procurator will not be here forever, and his successors are almost sure to be more reasonable. But once set on foot, war cannot easily be broken off or fought to a conclusion without disaster.

'As for your passion for liberty, it comes too late; you ought to have made a supreme effort to retain it long ago. For the experience of slavery is a painful one, and to escape it altogether any effort is justified; but the man who has once submitted and then revolts is a refractory slave, not a lover of liberty. Thus the time when we ought to have done everything possible to keep the Romans out was when the country was invaded by Pompey. But our ancestors and their kings, with material, physical, and mental resources far superior to yours, faced a mere fraction of the Roman army and put up no resistance; will you, who have learnt submission from your fathers and are so ill provided compared with those who first submitted, stand up to the whole Roman Empire? . . .

'Where are the men, where are the weapons you count on? Where is the fleet that is to sweep the Roman seas? Where are the funds to pay for your expeditions? Do you think you are going to war with Egyptians and Arabs?

Look at the far-flung empire of Rome and contrast your own impotence. Why, our forces have been worsted even by our neighbours again and again, while their arms have triumphed over the whole world! ...

'It is terrible to be enslaved it will be said. How much worse for Greeks, who surpass every nation under the sun in nobility and fill such a wide domain, and yet bow before the fasces of a Roman governor ...

'But if any people might reasonably be tempted to rebel by its peculiar advantages, that people is the Gauls, provided as they are with such marvellous natural defences, on the east the Alps, on the north the Rhine, on the south the Pyrenees, on the west the Ocean ...

'Consider the defences of the Britons, you who feel so sure of the defences of Jerusalem. They are surrounded by the Ocean and inhabit an island as big as this continent; yet the Romans crossed the sea and enslaved them, and four legions keep that huge island.

'Almost every nation under the sun bows down before the might of Rome; and will you alone go to war, not even considering the fate of the Carthaginians, who boasted of great Hannibal and their glorious Phoenician ancestors, but fell beneath Scipio's hand? ...

'So there is no refuge left except to make God your ally. But He too is ranged on the Roman side, for without His help so vast an empire could never have been built up. Think too how difficult it would be, even if you were fighting feeble opponents, to preserve the purity of your religion, and how you will be forced to transgress the very laws which furnish your chief hope of making God your ally, and so will alienate Him. If you observe the custom of the Sabbath with its complete cessation of activity, you will be promptly crushed, as were your ancestors by Pompey, who was most active in pressing the siege on the days when the besieged were passive. But if in the war you transgress your ancestral Law I don't see what you have left to fight for, since your one desire is that none of your ancestral customs should be broken. How will you be able to call the Deity to your aid if you deliberately deny Him the service that is due?

'Everyone who engages in war relies on either divine or human help; but when, as is probable, both are denied, the aggressor is bringing certain destruction on himself. What prevents you from killing your wives and children with your own hands and from consigning your ancestral home, the most beautiful in the world, to the flames? By such madness you will at least avoid the shame of defeat! ...

'Again, the danger threatens not only ourselves here but also those who live in other cities: for there is not a region in the world without its Jewish colony. All these, if you go to war, will be massacred by your opponents, and through the folly of a few men every city will run with Jewish blood. There would be an excuse for such a massacre; but if it did not take place, think how wicked it would be to take up arms against such a kindly people!...

'... if you make a right decision you will share with me the blessings of peace, but if you are carried away by your passions you will go without me to your doom.' (*The Jewish War*).

*   *   *

But the people shouted out that they did not want to wait until Nero deigned to recall Florus. They wanted an end to it, to make war immediately. In fact had not the war already begun? They had just learned that Menahem and his men had taken the fortress of Masada from the Romans, having killed everyone in the garrison, and were marching on Jerusalem heavily armed. Rumour increased that Menahem was the Messiah of Israel. He entered Jerusalem where Agrippa and a few of his followers and a Roman cohort were besieged. Menahem's men were well supplied with light arms, but they did not find any heavy arms in the arsenal of Masada. It would be difficult to bring down the walls of the Antonia fortress, and the royal palace. Menahem had a tunnel dug, and his troops burst up into the interior of the stronghold. Agrippa II and his Jewish troops surrendered and were not unduly worried. But the Romans continued to hold out in the hope of intervention on the part of Gallus. All the same, their situation became untenable and they parleyed. Finally they surrendered, but according to Josephus they were all killed by Menahem's men, except for their commander, who promised to have himself circumcised. Jerusalem was Jewish once more. Suddenly the air was more pure there, the light more clear, and the horizon more distinct. Jerusalem breathed in liberty. Beneath the Temple, happiness slowly consumed seriousness, and the priests forgot the majesty of their sacred office. Laughter burst out in the galleries, and in the outer courts. The merchants felt younger, women looked at each other as in the spring of creation. Liberty was tangible, everyone clung to it with emotion.

With measured steps a crowd of Jews went up to the Temple. Menahem had put on the royal vestments and walked at the head of his armed men. Behind them were the inhabitants of Jerusalem. Menahem seemed to be pursuing a destiny that was beyond him. He crossed the Court of the Gentiles and went towards the altar. He was the liberator of the city, the man who had driven out the Romans and brought the nation to the eve of the war against the occupier. He came to meet his God and have himself recognized as His envoy. 'Look to yourselves, Sons of Darkness, the Sons of Light are marching against you.' Menahem spoke like the Messiah. He was still moving towards the sacred precinct. Then there was complete silence. The people stopped as if they did not want to take part in the sacrilege. The young priests were together at the entry to the portico and made a barrier with their bodies. The followers of the son of Judas the Galilean realized that the people refused to recognize their leader as the envoy, the saving Messiah. They instinctively drew back as the first stone hit Menahem. The men who had driven out Gallus, and given back to Jerusalem the liberty that had been lost for over a century, fled towards Masada as the man that Israel did not want for king tottered.

As soon as these extraordinary events were known throughout the Empire, tens of thousands of Jews were massacred, in all the cities, from Damascus to Alexandria, from Caesarea to Askalon, as if resistance to Rome and a temporary victory against the Roman occupiers were a sacrilege. The Greeks, Egyptians and Syrians could not bear that the Jews should succeed where they had failed. Cestius Gallus, the Roman governor, was already preparing to march on Jerusalem.

*   *   *

With a very strong army Gallus entered Judaea and easily made himself master of the coastal strip, then of the whole of Galilee.

It was the Feast of the Tabernacles, and most of the Jewish nation was in Jerusalem. On this holy day the news of the advance of the Roman governor reached the Jews. Then, for the first time in their modern history, they left the Temple and its ceremonies and rushed out to meet the Romans. The fight was extremely violent. The invaders were surprised by the keenness and warlike spirit of the Jews. They retreated, but a few days later they arrived at the gates of Jerusalem and camped on Mount Scopus, which dominates the Holy City. After five days of prevarication Gallus sent in his troops, who advanced as if they were on parade, in combat ranks. The Jews were frightened by this tactic, abandoned the city and took refuge in the Temple. Gallus hesitated. Feebly, he tried to manoeuvre his troops into the sanctuary which Pompey had once violated. The resistance was desperate. Then Gallus raised the siege and set off towards Syria without anyone knowing why. The Jews followed and inflicted considerable losses. Then an immense silence fell on Jerusalem.

The Jewish people looked into their souls and once more took measure of the depth of their destiny.

The Jewish nation had arrived at a great moment patiently prepared by the Zealots and the *sicarii*, mystically foreseen and wished for by the Essenes, intellectually accepted by the Pharisees and feared by the Sadducees. It was war. Since the Jews had defeated Gallus, the Romans could not sit still, or else they would lose the whole of Asia; and Nero was not the man to accept that sort of defeat.

This time there was no doubt that war would follow.

3 The Battle of Galilee

Simon ben Gamaliel strode through the corridors of the Temple in Jerusalem. He had just obtained—from the Sanhedrin council of war—supreme authority for the direction of operations. The entire burden of this impossible war against Rome was to fall on his shoulders, but the responsibilities did not frighten him. What really did worry him was the frivolity and the lack of awareness of his colleagues. In spite of the immediate danger they had saddled him—a Pharisee—with Hanan, a confirmed Sadducee, as adjutant, a man who manifestly wanted to treat the Romans with respect. Political intrigue had won the day.

The Sanhedrin continued in unbroken session night and day in the Hall of Carved Stone. The doors opened and closed with a din. Breathless riders from Sepphoris and Gamala, Tiberias or Jotapata threw their messages on to the marble table and ran out. There was time for no more than a glance at them. For the present the pace of the debate had slowed down because the Sanhedrin was going to draw up a battle order and assign the commands of the various zones for the defence of the territory. Intrigue was rife, and compromise followed compromise. Eventually the extremist candidates were eliminated, and both local and general direction of the operations were given to men who were known to be prudent.

But every member of the Sanhedrin was wondering who ought to be given the responsibility for the defence of the vital region of Galilee, through which the enemy offensive would be bound to pass. Names were put forward and rejected. The debate went on endlessly. Then the High Priest, Joshua ben Gamala, spoke: 'Galilee must have a first-rate man who is brave and knows the province well. I propose Josephus.' The Josephus referred to was Flavius Josephus, the future author of the only complete historical testimony we have to this period. In 66 he was still called Josephus ben Mattathias, and it was only much later, round about 75, that he took—in honour of the Flavian dynasty—the name under which he passed into history: Flavius Josephus.

There was unanimous surprise.

That evening Josephus bolted his door and shut himself in his house. His usual nonchalance gave way to feverishness. Before dawn he would know whether or not he was to be Governor of Galilee. A friend was to bring him the news, whether it be good or bad, and at no matter what time of night.

Josephus knew that his career would depend on the Sanhedrin's decision. He was only twenty-eight. He was obsessed with a desire to do something. The three years of mortification he had spent in the desert with an obscure Essene hermit had certainly afforded him a rich mystical experience. But to what purpose? It was politics that really excited him. Josephus became aware of the fact when he was in Rome, bargaining to save some Jewish priests who had been arrested by Felix and who were threatened with heavy sentences on flimsy charges. The success he had had with Empress Poppaea, a distant and implacable woman, convinced him of his skill in manoeuvring and his gifts for diplomacy.

In the silence of his room, Josephus weighed his chances, estimating the interplay of forces between his supporters and his opponents in the council. The minutes went by. He waited, his nerves on edge.

The mere mention of Josephus' name was enough to arouse the passions of the Sanhedrin. Was this young nobleman with his refined education really qualified to lead the struggle against the invading armies to the bitter end? On his return from Rome, had he not publicly expressed his admiration for the Imperial civilization and institutions? 'It is all slander,' said Joshua ben Gamala. 'The man I propose as Governor of Galilee is a young, patriotic leader. Do not forget that his mother was a descendant of our own Hasmonaean kings, the very rulers who once gave us back our independence and our pride.' The prestige of the high priest resolved any hesitations. When the lights in the Temple were extinguished, Josephus had won.

Somewhere in Galilee, a group of militant Zealots were assembled with their leader when the news arrived that the Sanhedrin had appointed Josephus as governor of the province—someone completely unknown as far as the resistance was concerned. The sympathy of these fighting men was naturally with the man who inspired their resistance, John of Gischala, who was extremely popular with the Galilean people. He had dark hair, a lean figure, craggy face and deep black eyes, was of medium height and had a calm nature. He had given up an easy life for revolt and insurrection. An intelligent man, he had voluntarily gone underground and, well before war broke out, had formed guerilla groups in the mountains whose exploits against the Roman legions or their Jewish collaborators had fired the Galileans with enthusiasm.

John and his followers were indignant when they heard that the moderates had been successful in securing the key posts in the national defence. The Sanhedrin had eliminated the patriots. John of Gischala's reply was to give the order for systematic agitation. He exposed himself to danger. He was seen everywhere, like some tireless commercial traveller for God and Liberty. With feverish activity he nourished the flame of resistance, organizing meetings and discussions in the towns and countryside. There were Roman agents everywhere, but he hunted them mercilessly, struggling to contradict their whispered propaganda, and bringing down the most troublesome of them.

Mobilization was accelerating everywhere. Volunteers were enlisting *en masse* in response to his call to the people's militia: former officers and men of Agrippa's army; fishermen from the Lake of Tiberias, and hardened members of the underground who had already made considerable trouble for the regular Roman soldiers. In Jerusalem there was warlike enthusiasm. Fanatical boys and girls, singing all the time, strengthened the walls, made spear heads and swords, designed and built heavy weapons, or repaired, as best they could with the materials available, those captured from the Romans. John was not only worried about the modern equipment and the power of the Roman legions. He was alarmed by the manoeuvres of betrayal from inside. The country was littered with foreign communities whose attitude towards the Romans gave cause for serious concern. Roman troops who had been forced off their route by the resistance were quite often helped, when they moved forward again, by non-Jewish peoples who generally rallied to the occupying power. In any case Samaria, the province between Galilee and Jerusalem, was well and truly occupied by Rome, thus constituting a permanent menace to Jewish communications. The enemy controlled almost the entire Mediterranean coast, and had scattered the area with colonies and fortresses. Concentrations of troops could therefore move along the coastal territory, from Syria as far as Egypt, without risk.

*   *   *

This dangerous strategic situation had not escaped the attention of the supreme council in charge of the ultimate command of the regular Jewish forces. They called a young officer from the general staff because his

Essene affiliation was, in the eyes of the Sanhedrin, guarantee of absolute devotion to the cause of independence. The determination and frankness of the man had already made a deep impression on Simon ben Gamaliel and the other rulers of Jerusalem.

John the Essene spoke: 'The capture of Askalon must be our first objective. It is a small Mediterranean port near Gaza, but it controls all communications between the Roman forces in the north and those in the south. But we must strike quickly and decisively.'

The operation was immediately set in motion. The next day three detachments of Jewish soldiers moved towards the town with extraordinary speed. John the Essene was counting on the element of shock, as well as a Jewish uprising against the garrison. But in the middle of the night a spy ran from Jerusalem and roused the Roman commander.

'The Jews will attack in a few hours time.'

A general alert was ordered, but the commander remained calm.

'Let them come,' he told his officers. 'When they get near to Askalon they will be exhausted and we will beat off their attack.'

During the early part of the morning the Jewish troops reached the fortifications and prepared for the assault. Suddenly a considerable cavalry force, heavily armed, burst out of the town, and the Jews had only infantry to counter them with. When the Roman squadrons charged they were irrepressible and caused chaos in the Jewish ranks. The battle raged for hours. By evening the Jews, besieged by the cavalry and the legions, were forced to retreat. John the Essene was killed and ten thousand Jewish corpses lay on the battlefield.

*   *   *

The failure of the operation was taken badly. Strategy had to be modified. Joshua ben Gamala explained to the supreme council that the battle of Jerusalem was inevitably going to be fought in Galilee. 'I congratulate myself,' he said, 'on having directed your choice to Josephus for the defence of the province. The key to Jerusalem is in good hands.'

Everyone looked towards Galilee and its new governor. Everywhere able bodied men were mobilized, trained and armed. Josephus tightened the discipline of the Jewish troops and introduced trumpet signals for attack and retreat. The soldiers learned the art of thwarting the tactical manoeuvres of the Roman commanders. One hundred thousand keen men were on war footing, supported by a people determined to win.

But although the Galileans had confidence in their governor, John of Gischala and his men had few illusions about the determination and inner convictions of the aristocrat with the delicate hands. Of course he had showed energy and initiative from the very outset of his mission; but was he really involved heart and soul in the struggle? Wasn't he trying to gain time, to restrain the uprising, nurture every possibility of a compromise with Rome, and avoid at all costs a general revolt which might well become a social revolution? John of Gischala's fears were quickly realized. His agents informed him that Josephus had had secret contacts with the agents of Agrippa II, and that he had even gone as far as asking for massive Roman intervention and the suppression of extremist conspiracies. Josephus' double dealing was confirmed when it was learned that the stronghold of Sepphoris, some twenty or so miles from Tiberias, was now entirely in the hands of the pro-Roman party, and that it had seceded and gone over to the enemy.

A few days later a caravan escorted by royal agents and carrying a large amount of treasure crossed Galilee to enter territory occupied by Roman troops. Resistance fighters attacked the convoy, took away the treasure and gave it to Josephus, who solemnly promised that it would be sent to the defenders of Jerusalem. But scarcely had the resistance turned their backs than Josephus hastened to return it surreptitiously to its owners. But the secret soon leaked out. An angry crowd rushed towards the governor's house. An implacable Josephus invited a delegation to come and talk with him, and maintained that the people had been misled by lies. 'I will give you the treasure back immediately,' he said. A few men went into the house. Instantly Josephus had them seized and atrociously tortured. One was set free with one of his severed hands hung around his neck.

John of Gischala exploded with rage and decided to go himself and demand an explanation from Josephus. Despite the advice of his followers who recommended discretion, and feared an ambush, he appeared in the governor's camp. He looked at the soldiers round Josephus' tent. They were brave, but they were dazzled by the prestige of a man who was secretly preparing them for slavery. Sentries took him to Josephus, who icily awaited the impact. The confrontation began. On the one hand was the sceptical, insinuating aristocrat, and on the other the intrepid, militant revolutionary. John came straight to the point:

'The people demand that military preparations be speeded up and that Roman agents be rendered harmless. The town of Gischala must be

fortified and supplied with the wheat that the procurators hastily abandoned in some of the villages of upper Galilee.' John demanded an account
of the barbaric treatment his envoys had just received. 'When are we to
believe you? When you organize the resistance, or when you have the
best Jewish fighters tortured?' Josephus was not lost for a reply. He used
subtle arguments and fine words, and referred to his efforts to ensure that
the territory was defended. John became more insistent, and demanded
material evidence. Josephus revealed his true intentions. In guarded terms
he alluded to a compromise peace which would save Judaea from certain
defeat. 'I refuse to deal with agents of subversion and disorder.' John of
Gischala understood. There was no possibility whatsoever of reconciliation
between the two men.

    John went back to his men. Encouraged by the support of the Zealots
and the fact that many cities that had decided to fight, he addressed a
report to the council in Jerusalem. They would have to decide one way
or the other in the serious struggle in which Galilee was at stake. After a
confused debate between Josephus' enemies and friends, the council came
out against him, and ordered him to resign his office. But was Josephus
going to accept the verdict without a struggle? He at once slandered John
maliciously and accused the rulers in Jerusalem of corruption. The council
replied by appointing four commissioners to cover the whole of Galilee
and incite the population to ignore Josephus' orders. As a precaution two
thousand five hundred men were mobilized to protect the commissioners,
and prevent any violence from the suspended governor. Josephus not only
stuck to his position, but assembled thousands of mercenaries under his
command. As soon as the commissioners arrived in Galilee, they sent a
young soldier to Josephus with a message calling on him to attend a
meeting. Josephus was dining when the rider arrived. He took the letter
but did not open it. Suddenly he had an idea. 'Why not make this soldier
confess that his superiors are luring me into a trap in order to kill me?'
Smiling broadly, he offered the man a glass of wine, then a second, a third
and a fourth. Soon the timid soldier was blind drunk and launched into
incredible admissions. The next morning Josephus wrote his reply and
gave it to the man, who had completely forgotten the folly of the previous
night. Josephus announced throughout the province that Jerusalem wanted
to murder him.

    In the face of such bad faith the council at Jerusalem decided to
have the town of Tiberias occupied by their troops. Tiberias was the
capital of Galilee, and in this way Josephus would be deprived of any

possible means of resisting superior orders. The operation was carried out quickly and the soldiers of the central authority made a triumphal entry into the town without a hint of resistance.

Josephus was at Jotapata, north of Sepphoris, and a day's march from Ptolemais, when the news reached him of Jerusalem's latest show of authority. He would have to decide whether or not he was to let himself be intimidated by this operation. Although he had been disappointed by the lack of response on the part of the people of Tiberias, and their passivity in the face of occupation by the soldiers from Jerusalem, he knew that the balance of power was in his favour. He also thought that if he were to retake Tiberias there would be no violent reaction from a Sanhedrin that was in any case in revolt and only too happy to have a line of defence against Vespasian, even if Josephus was in command of it.

Tiberias was besieged and Josephus lost no time in launching his offensive against the members of the council at Jerusalem. The town was sacked and the troops loyal to the council fled in disorder. Mounds of corpses strewed the path of the governor's procession as he made his entry once more into his capital city. Blood had been shed, but Josephus had re-established his old authority. From now on he would be able to treat with Jerusalem on equal terms. The business would be even more simple since, it would appear, the Romans were about to launch their formidable attack.

The council at Jerusalem found itself unceremoniously confronted by the dissidence of a great leader who scoffed at its orders and was determined to pursue his own policies. Simon ben Gamaliel proposed full retaliation, but the council was divided against itself and let the matter drop.

*   *   *

The whole of Greece was witnessing with some amazement the eccentricities of a famous guest, the Roman Emperor. Nero, at thirty years of age, was disgusted at the coarseness and lack of understanding of his subjects. He thought that only civilized people—in this case the Greeks—were capable of appreciating his talents for art and sport. The trip was beyond all expectations. At Olympia Nero took part in a chariot race. He was beaten by several lengths after an unlucky fall, but he was still proclaimed victor. Fortune was certainly smiling on him. The emperor became bolder. He displayed himself in the theatres, played in comedies, sang, recited verse and strummed the lyre. The good public acclaimed him, but under somewhat special conditions. Out of respect for the master singer of the world it was thought wise to forbid any spectator to leave the auditorium during the course of the performance.

But pleasure was short lived. The applause rained down, but then so did the bad news. While he admired his prizes and his trophies, Nero heard that a vague and fanatical tribe in Judaea had apparently dared to revolt against the legions of Rome. Nero had the very man in his entourage who could bring the revolt to heel. General Flavius Vespasian was still rather surprised to have his head left on his shoulders. He had in fact only just escaped the death penalty for *lèse majesté* for falling asleep during one of Nero's performances. Nero never trifled when marks of respect were involved, but in this case he had contented himself with striking the general's name off the army list. However, when events pressed him, Nero immediately appointed the unemployed general—and for once did so with little rancour. He did it all the more quickly since fantastic rumours were flying about among his entourage. They were saying that the Jewish match was liable to set the eastern powder magazine alight, and that Judaea was not only intent upon getting rid of Rome, but of enslaving the whole world.

Vespasian had a calm face, a bald skull and was fifty-seven years old. He had three children, one of whom was Titus. He was the grandson of one of Pompey's centurions and the son of a tax-collector in whose honour several Asian cities had erected statues with the inscription, 'To the publican, an honest man.' Vespasian was a very composed Roman, proud of his origins, who had won his stripes with the fist. He loathed pomp and aristocrats. One day he violently scolded some servile courtiers who came and whispered in his ear, 'We have been making investigations. Did you know that you were descended from Hercules?'

All the same, he did not escape the slander of the nobility. Vespasian was a miser. His wife was the former mistress of a Roman lord. Had he not been a horse-dealer?

*   *   *

The year 67 began. Vespasian left Greece with no idea of what he'd find in the East, ravaged as it was by burning passions. He crossed Asia, then decided to install his headquarters and his services in the Mediterranean port of Ptolemais, now St John of Acre (Akko). The general-in-chief had tens of thousands of men, cavalry and infantry, with Arab and Lebanese reinforcements sent by local sovereigns who had been domesticated by Rome.

Vespasian lost no time. His army was on war footing and he put on a state of alert his network of secret agents, some of whom had succeeded in infiltrating the ruling circles in Jerusalem. Then the general drew up his strategy in great detail. In his estimation the mistake which was not to be made was that of attacking Jerusalem prematurely. It would be easy, when the resistance of the provinces had been dealt with, to deal the final blow to an isolated demoralized fortress which was cut off from outside support.

There were plenty of distractions at Ptolemais. Feasts and receptions came one after the other. All the vassal kings, perspiring with fear, crowded into the general-in-chief's camp, wearing themselves out with homage and flattery. They presented their reports, gave information, took orders, and went away consoled or uneasy, according to whether the master had delivered a compliment or a reprimand.

In this festival of servility there was one who was doing his apprenticeship in the understanding of men, diplomacy and leadership. It was Vespasian's son Titus, then aged twenty-six. Titus had been brought up in Nero's entourage and was a close friend of Britannicus. He had been covered in favours by the gods. He had unusual physical vigour, an open and sympathetic face, wide knowledge of Greek and Latin culture, a marked taste for eloquence, music and poetry. He also had a rather unusual social talent of being able to write extremely quickly and imitate the signatures of his fellows with consummate skill.

Even so, Vespasian had not been able to prevent his son from leading the idle life, from taking part in debauches with the gilded youth of Rome, and for marrying twice. Exasperated by the many scandals, Vespasian sent his son to fight in Britain and in Germania, then had brought him along to Judaea to keep an eye on him. Scarcely had he arrived in Ptolemais than the young officer noticed a beautiful Jewish princess of high rank. It was Berenice, the daughter of Agrippa I. She was thirteen years older than Titus, but few were able to guess her age. Titus could not resist her seductive qualities. In the midst of a full-scale war a madly passionate love affair began. In the arms of Titus, Berenice forgot the past, her first marriage to the King of Chalkis, the outburst of popular joy that greeted the death of her husband, and above all the circumstances of her second marriage. Rumour accused Berenice of having had an incestuous relationship with her brother, and she was therefore resigned, in order to discredit it, to marrying the mediocre King of Cilicia. No one among the Roman aristocracy was fooled.

The Roman steam-roller went into action. First of all Vespasian occupied a certain number of the fortresses on the west frontier, then moved on the town of Gamara which the Jews had decided not to defend so as to be able to carry out guerilla actions. Vespasian scarcely met any resistance, but this did not prevent him from ordering a terrible massacre of the people.

The Roman army left Gamara in flames, and moved towards its new objective, the stronghold of Jotapata, a few miles away. Josephus was there, abandoned by the popular leaders and no longer having an organized force in the country. He now represented only himself, but worked hard at the role which he thought he could still play as intermediary between Rome and Jerusalem. In a message to Jerusalem he wrote: 'If you wish to deal with the enemy, let me know as quickly as possible. If you insist on making war, send me the troops necessary to fight.'

The Roman troops met their first difficulties, for everything had been taken into account in the energetic defence of a town whose situation was of great strategic importance. On the hilly roads which led to Jotapata, the Jews constructed formidable obstacles to slow down the advance of the cavalry and the heavy enemy war machines. But with the prolonged efforts of Vespasian's sappers, the army succeeded in crossing this area and drawing up before the ramparts. From the top of the war machines arrows, javelins, blocks of stone and flaming torches rained down on the besieged. There were numerous assaults. One evening a rumour flew round the Roman camp that Vespasian had been wounded. An arrow had hit the general in the foot.

The days went by. While there was no lack of provisions inside the city, tension was mounting. Water was scarce, and the suffocating June heat flattened the soldiers and inhabitants. On July 1 Vespasian, who was well informed about the horrible conditions inside the town, gave Titus the order to decimate the city. There was a horrific manhunt through the underground and caves in which the defenders had taken refuge. Forty thousand victims, women and children, died in the attack. But in Jerusalem they said that the victory was of no significance. The town had been taken by treachery.

*　　*　　*

Silence fell on the martyr city of Jotapata in which resistance had ceased. In the middle of the night a man descended the slopes of the fortress. It was Josephus who, throughout the siege, had taken part either willingly or against his will, in the defence of Jotapata. He was followed by forty militiamen who had escaped the slaughter. They were silent, and alive to the slightest noise. They disappeared into a cave where they knew they would find provisions for a few days.

The next day a woman pointed out to the Roman commander that Josephus had disappeared, but that he had not left Jotapata. A search was organized and the hiding place was soon discovered. Vespasian realized that Josephus would make a splendid prisoner-of-war. He immediately chose a member of his general staff and sent him to parley with Josephus. The Roman was clever and flatteringly insinuated that if Josephus would give himself up, Vespasian would appreciate his worth and would negotiate with him. From the back of the cave Josephus savoured the promises made to him. As soon as his companions realized that he was going to succumb to the Roman flattery they became very angry.

'You want to live at any price. Not us. You are going to follow our example and behave like a true Jewish leader. If you refuse we will kill you as a traitor.'

Josephus had no wish to die there, in that hole, for a cause he hated. He spoke to them at length, interminably, quoting the commandments of the Jewish Law which forbade suicide, but it was no use. Then Josephus suddenly accepted their plan. Two men would be chosen by lot. The first would kill the second, then the second would be killed by the third and so on. Gradually the number of corpses in the cave increased. Thirty-nine men were now dead. There was only Josephus and a soldier. Would Josephus kill the man and then commit suicide, or vice versa? By means of persuasive words on the joys of life, Josephus managed to dissuade the man.

'But if I give myself up,' the unhappy man asked, 'What will the Romans do to me?'

'I will take care of that,' replied Josephus. 'I will speak on your behalf.'

Josephus could breathe once more. He went out of the cave. The officer took him in charge and escorted him to Vespasian. The emperor's embarrassment outdid his satisfaction. What was he going to do with this prisoner? Should he send him to Rome and leave it to Nero to determine his fate? Josephus observed this indecision and decided to take a risk. In his most solemn tone of voice he prophesied:

'One day you will be emperor, Vespasian, and Titus your son will succeed you on the throne.'

Vespasian withdrew to consider his alternatives.

'Josephus will be no use whatsoever in Rome. There is every advantage in keeping with me a man who knows his country's customs thoroughly. It is a country I am in the process of conquering and of which I know very little.'

Josephus would not be delivered to Nero. He was put in chains, but believed himself to be indispensable, and hoped that he would soon be free.

*   *   *

The Romans pushed further into Galilee. After the fall of Japha and the defeat of the defenders of Mount Gerizim in Samaria, Vespasian turned towards Joppa (Jaffa), between Gaza and Caesarea. This famous port was giving anchorage to a large Jewish fleet which, from Syria to Egypt, patrolled the coast, attacking Roman convoys, sinking them or taking their cargoes. Vespasian sent a big force against Joppa to deal with the garrison. The defenders took refuge on board their ships and stood off from the coast to avoid the deluge of missiles raining on the port. A terrible storm blew up, and the uncontrolled ships bumped into one another amid the heaving waves. On that day four thousand Jews died, either drowned or murdered on the coast.

A new centre of trouble was Tarichaeae, a strongly fortified fishing port on the edge of the Lake of Tiberias. The Jewish resistance was so strong that Titus had to ask for reinforcements. There was fighting on the lake and on land, but the superior number of men weighed in favour of the Romans. Then there was a quarrel inside the city, between those who were for and those against surrender. When he heard about this, Titus appealed to his men.

'Comrades, now is the time. Don't hesitate, because God is on our side. Do you hear those shouts? Those who have escaped us are killing each other. We will capture the town if we take advantage of the present.' Once again Vespasian unleashed terror on the devastated town, over which hung an atrocious smell of putrefying bodies. Some six thousand prisoners were gathered together and sent to Corinth as forced labour.

Vespasian's men crossed the ruins and gathered up more than a thousand old people and children. The prisoners were marched off to an open area and slaughtered in the sight of a horrified crowd.

Slowly Galilee sank into servitude. As each day passed the isolation of Jerusalem became more apparent. One important objective still resisted the pressure of the Roman army, and that was Gamala. After a bloody battle this, too, was taken. The Romans who were now in control of the conquered towns gave no help to the miserable population who were without a leader and had given in to despair.

*   *   *

Jerusalem was in a state of extreme tension. The inhabitants realized that they could not count on any outside help. This feeling of isolation was not the only reason for anxiety. Thousands of Galilean refugees had literally invaded the city, telling of the horrors they had witnessed, circulating fantastic rumours and describing the formidable strength of the Roman forces.

Furthermore the rumour had it that Josephus had been killed under the debris of Jotapata. His life-long enemies were embarrassed by this news and tried to forget their hostile attitude towards him, since he now appeared to be a martyr to the Jewish cause. Thirty days' mourning was ordered. A weeping crowd of people marched in procession through Jerusalem, singing prayers and psalms. Then the truth became known. Although he was a prisoner, Josephus was in excellent health, and had all the respect due to his rank. The singing stopped, and the anger of the mob turned against the deserters' friends who still sat on the council. Josephus' betrayal of the cause seemed, to the Zealots, to justify their action. The time had come to take advantage of the people's hatred and use it against the moderate elements who still held the essential power.

The Council of Jerusalem now felt its authority slipping away. Its orders fell on thin air, and no one listened any more to their calls for prudence and calm. Under the influence of the Zealots a parallel power was set up and immediately taken over by the activists. The first batch of arrests included several important members of the aristocracy as well as the administrator of the public treasury, who were all accused of treason. Several days went by. The Zealots thought it a good moment for another big strike. They maintained that the aristocrats—even those already imprisoned—were still involved in outside machinations, and threatened the independence and freedom of the people. Ten men went into the cells and coldly murdered the prisoners.

The revolution had begun. The Zealots next attacked the religious institutions. The established order was essentially founded on a hereditary priesthood. A few noble families controlled this privilege. It was high time to make the office of sacrificer democratic.

In a farmyard a peasant was sitting on a box repairing a plough-share. Suddenly three richly dressed men appeared. They were from the Temple of Jerusalem.

'As of this morning,' said one of them, 'you are the High Priest of Israel. You are going to put on the high priest's vestments and come with us to Jerusalem where you will make your entry.'

'It must be a mistake. You have the wrong place. There is no high priest here.'

'Are you called Phanias?'

'Yes,' mumbled the peasant.

'Well then you can see that we are not mistaken.'

'But I am only a farmer.'

'Yes, we have just revived the ancient custom of having high priests chosen by lot. Now the humblest Jews will not be held back by the powerful.'

Phanias left his house and fields. Dressed in the priestly vestments, he set out for Jerusalem.

In the eyes of the resistance the council had become the weapon of the foreign party. The Zealots gathered on the fortified site of the Temple and prepared to confront the government troops. One morning the inevitable collision occurred. Stones and javelins were hurled for several hours, but the revolutionary day ended in failure. The Zealots withdrew behind the second wall of the Temple. Hanan, Governor of Jerusalem, refused to pursue his advantage and intended to save his troops for any eventual negotiations with Vespasian. His aim was to force the Zealots into submission rather than exterminate them. He was content to blockade them in the Temple with a small army of six thousand men, recruited from the population, and relieved periodically. But the system worked badly. The rich young men were very happy to argue with words, but they had little taste for taking up arms. For a financial consideration they preferred to have poor men do their duty for them.

The day after their failure, the ultra-Zealots took stock of the situation and came to the conclusion that the balance of power was in favour of the council. They were unable to break the blockade through their own means and decided to call for help from the Idumaean soldiers encamped near the city. Two brave soldiers succeeded in getting through the lines, introduced themselves to the Idumaeans and told them about the situation in Jerusalem. If the council won, the city would be handed over to the Romans and the rule of the procurators re-established. This skilfully delivered threat was enough to force a decision. Twenty thousand armed Idumaeans set off towards the city. The members of the council were panic-stricken and quickly had the city gates closed. One of them went up on to the ramparts and delivered a long speech to the Idumaean leaders in which he took pains to show how wrong the intentions attributed to the council by the Zealots were.

'Did not we proclaim the revolt ourselves, when we could have prevented it? For myself I would have preferred peace, but the war is on now, and it continues. I prefer death to slavery.' The harangue had no effect. The Idumaeans refused to go back to their camp and demanded that they be allowed to enter the city. The council hardened its position and increased the guard on the walls. One evening a large storm broke over Jerusalem. In the confusion the Zealots succeeded in forcing the gates without drawing attention to themselves. The Idumaeans poured into the city and with the help of the Zealots finally freed from the Temple, occupied the strategic points of Jerusalem. There was mad, pitiless slaughter. Hanan was killed in the name of the triumph of God and the people, along with most of the senior clergy.

The moderate government was dismembered and sank in blood. A committee of public safety emerged from the unrest and took over all the powers and exercised a patriotic and social dictatorship. The champions of the old regime were banished or summarily executed. Terror set in.

The Idumaeans, who had entered Jerusalem in the hopes of helping the Zealots to crush the pro-Roman party, were sickened by the merciless fanaticism of the extremists. They began to leave the city, but only when they had obtained the release of two thousand prisoners arbitrarily accused of collusion with the enemy.

During this crisis of confidence, John of Gischala recovered a great part of his authority over the people. However, on the west bank of the Dead Sea there was a fortress, Masada, which was controlled by Simon bar Giora, a man younger than John of Gischala, fiery, ambitious, and coldly passionate. When the council was overthrown, Simon thought the moment had come to seize power. He gathered considerable forces around him and with his followers took up his stand in the hilly regions, declaring his intention to fight Rome with renewed vigour. He was a democrat and a revolutionary, and relied on the poorer members of society. He obviously intended overtaking John of Gischala on the left, and moving towards the genuine transformation of social structures. His popularity and military strength continued to increase, and he planned to attack Jerusalem. The Zealots became anxious and vainly tried to block his way. Simon did not strike immediately because he did not feel that he was strong enough to besiege Jerusalem. He invaded Idumaea, and in spite of the Zealot guerillas at first rallied many local militiamen to his side.

In Jerusalem the priests and the aristocracy were deliberately doing everything and anything in their power against John of Gischala. In order to get rid of him they did not hesitate to establish contact with Simon bar Giora, and without considering the consequences of their action very closely, opened the city gates for him. Simon entered Jerusalem as a victor. The unavoidable confrontation with the troops of John of Gischala took place and civil war flared up once more. The outcome was indecisive.

*   *   *

Vespasian was being pressed by his officers, who had detailed information on the internal strife in Jerusalem, to attack the city at once. But Vespasian held out. 'If we attack Jerusalem they will patch up their differences at once, thanks to us. The Jews will turn all their forces against us, and those forces are still considerable. Leave them for the present. Each day that passes will be marked by the death of a good number of the people we would have to fight. Disorder will serve to reduce our enemy's army. God is a more skilful commander than I. He will be the person to give the Jews to us without a fight.'

Without thinking any more about Jerusalem, Vespasian carried on with his march across Judaea and occupied the town of Gadara, then Jericho, where he improved the fortifications. But in June 68 the news of the death of Nero reached him. Vespasian wisely stopped harrassing the capital and concentrated on occupying some of the most strategic points in the country.

In the streets of the Holy City the people were quivering with hope.

They had just heard that civil war had broken out in the Roman Empire. The day after Nero's violent death, the Praetorian Guard had proclaimed as emperor, Galba, a gouty aristocrat of seventy-three. As soon as he ascended the throne he demanded that all the people who had received gifts from Nero should give them back to the public treasury. Nothing more was needed to arouse the fury of the very same men who had not the slightest intention of paying. A month later, in the middle of the Forum, Galba fell under their blows. His successor was a former favourite of Nero, a dishonest banker deeply in debt named Otho.

The legions of the Rhine immediately set themselves against an emperor imposed by the Praetorians at Rome, and quickly proclaimed their general, Vitellius, emperor. He moved into Italy, crushed Otho's troops at Cremona and entered Rome, which he treated as an enemy city. Otho committed suicide and Vitellius imagined that he had won, but in the end it was another general who was going to win the race for power. Emperors could now be made elsewhere, and so Vespasian was proclaimed. The Danube legions rallied to him, hurried to Rome, and executed Vitellius.

The Jew's enemy was now at the head of the Roman Empire. Of course he let them go on asking him to be emperor for a long time before he undertook a task so fraught with danger, but the insistence, and even the threats, of his own army overcame all his reticence. Then the new master of the world—the fourth in a year—remembered a distinguished prisoner. The man who had predicted his accession to the throne was mouldering away in an imperial prison. Vespasian ordered him to be set free and a joyful Josephus came out of his jail.

Vespasian now wanted to finish with the Jews and Jerusalem. Josephus would be useful to him. On the whole the situation was very favourable to the Romans. By the end of 69, throughout all Herod's old empire, Jewish resistance had practically ceased. The Romans were in control of the coastal strip, Galilee, Samaria and Judaea. Only Jerusalem still held out. The new emperor did not want to leave a job unfinished, particularly since the Jews, in control of Jerusalem, believed that they had successfully resisted the Roman armies. They had refused offers of peace on several occasions, and they boasted of having beaten a Roman general on two occasions.

Vespasian decided to give to Titus the job of taking the Jew's Holy City. Meanwhile, inside the powerful walls, the Jews counted their dead in the disastrous Galilean campaign, and wondered whether they had merely lost one battle, or whether they had already lost the war.

Part Two

COLLAPSE

4 The People of the Diaspora fail to rally round

From the top of Mount Scopus Simon ben Giora sadly watched a wretched new convoy of people arriving in Jerusalem. The refugees had been converging on the Holy City for several weeks. There were former soldiers beaten by the Romans, badly wounded and spiritually embittered. They were followed by hunched-up women and puny, ignorant children who drove their skinny goats and cattle. They had come to seek the protection of the last Jewish army still capable of fighting. But each one knew—and Simon first and foremost—that the long procession of refugees had come to Jerusalem to seek the protection of the Temple. The Temple was always there, right in the middle of the city; it shone with a thousand lights and would continue to do so through eternity. Simon thought that Jerusalem had increased its population at least tenfold, and that soon, in spite of the accumulated stocks of food, famine would set in. Sacrifice would cease because there would be no animals to sacrifice, and sickness and death would hold sway in the city of David. But Simon and all the Jews still felt that God would not abandon them, and that a supernatural intervention would save the beloved people of the All-powerful. The Creator had never abandoned His own since the waves of the Red Sea parted to allow those who were leaving Egypt to cross over, before enveloping Pharaoh's men; since the Maccabees got rid of the Seleucids and God brought His presence back into the Temple—never in the moments when the survival of the Jews was threatened.

But if, without admitting it, Simon counted on Divine intervention, he could not stop himself from thinking about the formidable power represented by the Jews in the Diaspora—not only in the Roman Empire, but also on the other side of the Euphrates, in the Kingdom of Parthia. There were approximately two million Jews living in Herod's old empire, but Simon knew that there were also about one million of his fellow-countrymen living in Egypt, where they had been for some time. In fact one in eight of the inhabitants of this Roman province was Judaean in origin. In Syria and in Asia Minor there were another million of the followers of

Moses, not to mention the tens of thousands of Jews living in Mesopotamia, Media and Babylonia. Even in Rome, the capital of such a splendid empire, there were at least sixty thousand Jews, and some of them were rich and powerful.

There were about fifty-five million inhabitants of the Roman Empire, of whom roughly five million were children of Abraham. Simon doubtless knew that for every hundred people under the authority of Rome, almost ten were Jewish. If they all rose in revolt simultaneously, victory would be possible. But Simon also knew that Rome's idea of imperial authority did not encourage the Jews to revolt, for Rome always respected the religious liberty of each person throughout the Empire. Thus the war which had just ravaged Galilee, and had reached the gates of Jerusalem, did not cause a revolt among the Diaspora. What would happen to Jerusalem now that the blockade was tightening once again? From his observation point Simon possibly hoped that, encouraged by the difficulties entailed by Nero's succession, his brothers of the Diaspora would be able to intercede with the Senate for an honourable end to hostilities. Some of the Jews living in Rome were Roman citizens with considerable privileges. Perhaps they would be able to persuade the Senate to stop Vespasian, who was both seeking the highest office in the Empire and determined to put an end to matters with the Jews.

In Rome itself, the life of the Jews went on much as before. They were, to the average Roman, part of the landscape, and the Roman was much more concerned about the problems created by Nero's succession than by the war in Judaea. Most Romans believed that the Jews had always been in the city built on seven hills, without any real reason and with no aim other than that of survival. Rome was no more foreign to them than they were to Rome. The Jews were in fact like all citizens of Rome. They spoke Latin, wore togas and walked around in sandals. They were no better armed than all the other inhabitants of the city. In the narrow streets of Rome, where it was forbidden to ride chariots during the day, they went about their business, engrossed and attentive at one and the same time. At night, when the city—which had no public lighting —was in total darkness, they remained in the districts in which they lived. No Jews—even the rich ones—went to the great Roman banquets or drank in the popular taverns. There were no Jews out at night in the unsafe alleys where citizens would only venture forth preceded by a group of slaves carrying torches and clubs. The Jews did not eat or drink with the worshippers of stone gods. These religious taboos were enough to drive a wedge between the Romans and the sons of Judaea. But to the Jews of Rome, Judaea itself—their place of origin—must have seemed very far away. The proud but unsafe Roman houses of four or five storeys which rose up into the sky had nothing at all in common with the sturdy homes of Jerusalem, firmly placed on solid earth. In common with all inhabitants of Rome, the Jews feared two scourges: collapse of the houses and fire.

The average Roman did not often venture into the Jewish districts of the capital, of which Trastevere was the oldest. All the Jews arriving in Rome went there voluntarily—no one forced them to do so, and indeed the first Roman Jews had asked as a favour to be allowed to live together in a district which might be their own. The Jews not only lived there, but had there also their place of worship and a kind of permanent 'information centre', which gave them news of their fellow Jews of the Diaspora and in Judaea. The Jews were neither better nor worse favoured than the other inhabitants of Rome. In common with all other Romans, they had to draw their water from the public fountains, empty their refuse into the open sewers and warm themselves at braziers that were dangerous for their safety.

Many Jews were Roman citizens and there was nothing to distinguish them from other Romans. But they were given a dispensation from worship of the emperor, and this was a subject of some surprise to the Roman who was accustomed to regard worship of the ruling lord as the common denominator of the whole city. Moreover, Jews had the right to settle directly among themselves matters of marriage, inheritance and worship. The Roman Jews were fortunate that the law allowed them the right to worship their one God.

But not all the Jews living in Rome were Roman citizens. Many were simply foreigners passing through, pilgrims, in fact, and not subject to Roman law. Others were foreigners living in Rome with no thought of going back to their country. They sometimes acquired the right of citizenship which allowed them to live at the foot of the Capitol, as any other Roman, but which did not carry with it the privileges attached to the status of citizen of the Roman Empire, particularly where political rights were concerned.

*   *   *

The Roman army was getting ready to lay siege to Jerusalem. And in

their camp, which Simon bar Giora could not yet see from the top of
Mount Scopus, was King Agrippa II, whose political importance was
henceforth nil. In contrast to Simon, Agrippa already knew that the Jews
of the Diaspora would not come to the help of their mother country.
The Jews who were Roman citizens would not intercede in favour of
those in Judaea. Unlike Simon, Agrippa was a pure product of Rome.
He was born and brought up there, and had shared the pleasures and
games of the gilded youth of the city. But insofar as he was the son of
Agrippa the Great, he had nevertheless always looked to Judaea, the
kingdom which had been promised him. He knew the Roman Jews well,
their history and their political strength. In the midst of the Roman
legions, not far from Vespasian's tent, he thought about his easy youth
again, the pleasures of Rome, and wondered whether his dreams for the
future were threatened. The Jews of the Diaspora were in danger of
paying for the warlike madness of the Jews of Judaea. Agrippa himself
had drawn the attention of the Jews to this aspect of the question when
there was still time to avoid the worst. He had advised prudence and
emphasized that revolt would cause blood to flow throughout the Diaspora,
wherever Jews were established and thought themselves to be safe.

Agrippa remembered learning from his father the history of the
Jews who had come to Rome. Malicious people said that the first Jews
to settle in Rome were spies. Agrippa had often heard this accusation, as
well as other unpleasant stories about the Jews which humorists were fond
of telling and which slandered the morals of the followers of Moses.

The truth was that in about the year 160 the Maccabees, afraid that
the Syrians would return in force, sent a considerable deputation to the
Roman Senate to conclude a treaty of mutual aid and non-aggression
between Rome and Judaea. The Senate agreed. The need to be perfectly
informed about what was taking place in Rome was obviously important
to the Maccabees, and so agents were left behind in Rome whose job it
was to liaise with the Senate and act as diplomatic representatives. These
few Jews in Rome, forgotten by the Hasmonaeans, formed the first kernel
of the Jewish colony there. In the next century their number grew, reinforced by a few immigrants from Judaea, but never numbering more
than one or two thousand people.

Agrippa had always thought that these first Jews remained foreigners
at Rome, and that the true Judaeo-Roman union had not begun until
after Pompey's victory. Certainly Pompey loved triumph, and had been
greatly disappointed at not being able to bring back from Judaea a visible

God; but he made up for it by producing a considerable number of prisoners in Rome. In 61 the Roman crowd which saw his triumph did not hide its disappointment. Among all those conquered by Rome, only the God of the Jews, who had no form, did not appear in the triumphal procession of a victorious Roman general. The Roman-born Jews watching the procession were saddened at seeing thousands of their brothers enslaved. Young King Aristobulus was at their head, and they dragged the heavy chains along the Via Appia, suffering the gibes and laughter of the Romans. But they refused to bow down before the emblems and idols of the pagans.

The news quickly spread among the Jews that although Pompey had violated the Holy of Holies, the Temple had not been destroyed, and the Jewish nation continued to exist. But the Jewish citizens faced the immediate problem of how to save the men who were now being paraded to be sold as slaves. They knew they must buy the greatest possible number of these unfortunate people and set them free.

Unfortunately, the few Jews in Rome had not been able to build up large fortunes. Only a few hundred slaves could be bought for immediate liberation. As soon as a slave was freed he became, in the eyes of the law of Rome, a Roman citizen. In this way, after a few months of captivity, the prisoners of war who were vowed to a servile existence suddenly became equals of the masters of the greatest empire in the world.

Many Romans rushed to acquire this new merchandise. Jews were known to be intelligent, hard working and devoid of vices. Proud owners soon became disillusioned. These slaves were fanatics. They would eat only certain foods and fasted frequently. This diminished their aptitude for work. They spent one day of the week doing absolutely nothing. Even their intelligence was a disadvantage! For how could one have in one's own home men who understood everything, who were more informed than their masters, who studied, read and spoke several languages!

Very soon these slaves could be bought back at a rock-bottom price by other Jews, who were themselves former slaves. Others were liberated by their Roman masters who hoped to gain more from them as newly freed men than as over-zealous servants.

The Jews made a resounding entry into Roman society. Within three years they were the equals of the wealthiest Roman citizens. They were sober and hard working. They saved a little money and amassed a great deal of moral authority. Nor was their political role negligible. In fact they took their new position as Roman citizens very seriously, but all the same they were prudent in their choice, since they were well aware that they also carried their Jewish nationality with them. In this way the Jews remained unmoved by the great internal conflicts which shook Roman society. For example, they took no side in the famous conspiracy when Catiline tried to seize power with an egalitarian and anarchist political programme. Indirectly, however, the affair rebounded on them, for the Romans had long been suspicious of secret societies and foreign gatherings practising ceremonies of which they knew nothing—and the Jews represented the epitome of a society which was foreign to every Roman norm.

*   *   *

The entire province of Judaea had risen against Rome, during the war in Galilee, and this had profoundly affected the situation of the Jews in Rome. The status they enjoyed with the ruling class and Roman intellectuals had been reduced to nothing. There was one principle on which no one at Rome would budge, neither the rulers, the intellectuals, the well-to-do, the army, nor the people. All believed that Rome had a special role to play among the nations, that its power should—and would—extend over the whole earth. Everyone had to submit to its power, which was no dream, but a partially realized necessity. Therefore when all the nations were conquered, and only then, a dialogue might begin, a kind of confrontation of intellectual ideals. But all nations were born to servitude. Roman servitude, however, was not synonymous with destruction. When they were protected by Rome, the other nations would be able to develop their individual genius without offending the Roman ideal. Only once in their history had the Romans decided to destroy a nation who had resisted them. Carthage had thrown off the Roman yoke and Hannibal had waged total war.

Once again, Rome was persuaded that she ought to hold the entire world in her power and at that point launched a war of extermination. The Jewish people, in precisely that way, were now making war on Rome. The scaffolding had collapsed. This war would be a struggle to the death. In 69 it was in theory certain that Jerusalem would suffer the fate of Carthage. From then on the illusions of the Jews in Rome about their own influence and the role they were capable of playing in Roman society also crumbled. Naturally they would not be persecuted, but any intervention on behalf of their brothers in Judaea would be regarded as suspect.

In any case, action would have been useless since Nero, followed by everyone else, had decided that an end must be put to the Jewish revolt.

When the Romans heard the details of the battle of Galilee they were amazed. They had not expected such a fanatical resistance, nor such an energetic war from an Oriental nation. The Gauls or the Germans may well offer heroic resistance, but it was unnatural that the Jews should launch a war. The shock waves from the Judaeo-Roman war also had a considerable effect on the people. There were no anti-Jewish demonstrations, but rather a campaign of systematic denigration and slander. The Jews had bad breath, they were dirty, beggars, evil-smelling, and were match-sellers.

Among the middle class, who were always eager for gossip, the growing influence of the Jewish princess Berenice over Vespasian's son was denounced. Licentious jokes about circumcision were repeated. It was a distinctive sign, so they said, to stop the Jews from having sexual relations with Gentiles. There were ironies about the Sabbath, and the congenital incapacity of the followers of Moses to work more than six days at a time without renewing contact with the Divine Power. The middle class moreover frequently confused the Sabbath with a fast day. Many Romans were greatly astonished that Jews should abstain from all food on so many occasions, or refuse certain categories of food, unless it was because their nature was different from that of other men, and because certain dishes were intolerable for them. Forbidding pork was also taken to be an anomaly. The Jews were afraid of contracting through this animal the plague which had so often struck them: both them and the pigs. All the complaints against the Jews were summed up by saying that they were enemies of the human race and that all their practices prohibited them from having normal relations with the rest of humanity.

When Nero died in 68, the struggle for the succession and the civil war in Judaea did not encourage Jewish diplomacy in Rome. Moreover, Vespasian had a good chance of becoming emperor—in fact his legions had just proclaimed him thus—and he had left Judaea to get himself acknowledged as head of the Roman Empire.

The Jews in Rome, knowing how helpless they would be in the coming battle for Jerusalem, could only hope that Titus would behave as Pompey had done, and that once the city was taken, he would not touch the Temple, which would still continue its role as catalyst for the Jewish nation.

5 Jerusalem, Jerusalem!

The Roman soldier was the best soldier in the world. He wore a pair of woollen trousers that left his calves bare, and a long coat of brownish leather. Over his tunic he wore a breastplate which covered his chest and shoulders. The steel plates slid over each other, adapting themselves to the movement of his body. He wore a bronze helmet on his head, and on his feet sandals tied with strong leather thongs.

In the spring of 70, at Caesarea, there was a festive atmosphere. The tiny Mediterranean port was packed with noisy soldiers brought by Titus from Egypt, by sea and land. Patrols passed through the streets near the large marble palace. At the crossings of streets and on the quays people jostled each other, talked, quarrelled, and even came to blows over a girl or the price of a drink. But the scuffle was soon broken up by the centurions, the all-powerful officers who had risen from the ranks and could be recognised by the vine-stock that was their badge of office.

Outside the town eighty thousand soldiers—Romans, Arabs and Syrians—carried out exercises, marched to and fro, cleaned their weapons, ate and drank, played at dice or slept in the sun with their head on a shield. At the centre of their huge square camp, which was divided up into sections, the tents of animal skin were lined up and fitted out to take ten men each. All the openings in the fortification were guarded by sentries, who were relieved at fixed intervals. At night it was wiser not to go near the camp. Mounted soldiers did the rounds from post to post to make sure that none of the soldiers had fallen asleep. The punishment for doing so was death.

In his headquarters Titus held many meetings so as to speed up the preparations for departure. Close to him was the head of general staff, Tiberius Alexander, a converted Jew, a former Roman procurator in Judaea and now a famous leader fanatically devoted to the Flavian dynasty. Then there was Josephus, the inseparable counsellor, who never left his prince and was going to guide the Roman army to the heart of his own country.

Three trumpet calls sounded in the camp at Caesarea. On the first the soldiers gathered up their weapons and dismantled their tents. On the second they loaded them on to pack animals, set fire to the camp so that it would be no use to an enemy, and on the third they set off. Each man carried a spear, a sword, and a four-sided oblong shield with a protuberance designed to repel missiles. In a basket he carried a saw, a sickle, an axe, a pick, a billhook, leather thongs, and bread for three days.

The army set off at dawn on an April day in the direction of Samaria. In front were the auxiliary troops provided by the vassal kings, then the sappers responsible for clearing the road. Then came Titus, escorted by crack troops, and the cavalry followed by countless siege machines. For several days the legions went forward in rows of six, always on the alert, exploring every inch of the terrain, ready for guerrilla action launched by Jewish desperadoes. Their objective was Jerusalem.

*   *   *

Perched on a hill 2,240 feet high, Jerusalem resembled a citadel rather than a city. On the side facing the Valley of Jehoshaphat, as on the side facing the south, the walls were several hundreds of feet high, and had a series of sharply-angled spurs and re-entrants so that in the event of a siege the enemy would always be exposed on his flanks. Enormous blocks of stone some sixty feet in length were jointed together by courses of lead and iron clamps. Along the ramparts there were a hundred and sixty-four square towers, with spiral staircases, from which the areas round about could be scanned. The Temple itself, with a double *enceinte*, constituted a powerful fortress. Through well-planned internal arrangements the various districts served as individual strongholds placed one next to the other. The approaches to the city were virtually impossible because of the series of ravines and precipices.

The permanent population had sharply increased, due to the tens of thousands of miserable refugees who had come from all parts of occupied Judaea. The revolutionary council, realizing that there would be a siege, had assembled large quantities of wheat and food and had turned houses, store places, and underground passages into public barns; but fires during the civil war had destroyed the larger part of the stocks. With the great moment of testing about to come, Jerusalem had no more time left to fill these irreparable gaps.

The Romans were pressing ahead, but there was no serious organization of the defences of Jerusalem. The political struggles still went on in their absurd, incoherent way. John of Gischala, who had the larger resources, held the lower town, and Simon ben Giora the upper town. Eleazar ben Simon controlled both the Temple and the Antonia fortress. He was the man who had refused to offer sacrifice in the Roman emperor's honour when he was Captain of the Temple. Even when the enemy was at the very gates of the city, these three armed factions still continued to indulge in bloody skirmishes in which they lost their best fighters.

It was the Eve of the Passover, John of Gischala had just been informed that on the actual feast day Eleazar was going to open the gates of the Temple to the faithful. John immediately called an élite group of his followers together in the utmost secrecy. 'The enemy is threatening us. We can no longer permit Eleazar's men to paralyse our efforts at organization and defence. Tomorrow we must take the Temple. My orders will be relayed to you tonight.'

The next day John's soldiers slipped into the Temple among the hundreds of pilgrims, with their weapons hidden under their clothing. They took up the positions which had been assigned them before hand, their hands clutching the hilt of their swords. When the signal was given they threw off their cloaks, drew their swords, and threw themselves on Eleazar's men, who were taken completely unawares. The key points in the Temple were taken in the fierce fight. Eleazar was captured, and that same evening most of his men went over to the victor. John of Gischala now emerged as the real mind behind the national resistance, and he was already thinking of his other, more disturbing rival, Simon ben Giora.

Enough Jewish blood had already been shed in the course of the monstrous struggles. John proposed an immediate meeting in which he and Simon could reveal their intentions. Very soon the whole of Jerusalem knew the time and place fixed for the meeting. A wave of enthusiasm and hope swept through the population. Negotiations began and impromptu speakers perched on chariots shouted slogans for brotherhood, watchfulness and determination. 'We have squandered our forces long enough. Unless our quarrels cease the enemy will take our city without having to spill a drop of blood.' Shouts of agreement came from all sides. Encouraged by weeping women, John's soldiers reached out towards those of Simon. Hands stretched out and clasped each other. Now the twenty-four thousand men were one single group, supported by a united people. Their fear was gone.

*   *   *

The Romans were now three miles from Jerusalem. Titus was eager to find a good site for his camp and carried out a reconnaissance operation. With six hundred cavalry beside him and wearing neither helmet nor breastplate, he rode into the suburbs of the city. A Jewish sentry signalled their approach. A desperate sally isolated Titus from his men, and despite the abilities of his horse he was unable to re-join them because the terrain was broken up with hedges, walls and piles of stones. Armed only with his sword, he fought through a hail of arrows. Finally a few Roman horsemen succeeded in surrounding him and brought him back to camp. Perspiring and still trembling, Titus rested. He mentioned only that the Jewish troops were more skilful and more cunning than had been expected. His officers took heed of the warning.

From the top of the walls of Jerusalem the sentries saw a strange kind of activity in the Roman camp. Clusters of soldiers were scattered across the space which separated Mount Scopus from the city walls. Shovels, picks and axes were out. Orchards were cut down, large trees rooted up, garden fences torn down and ravines filled in. When the soldiers went away there was nothing left of the rich area of cultivation outside Jerusalem. Across the large wasteland that had been created, men and machines could now be sent forward without difficulty. The best troops took up their positions in a square. The infantry were in front, and immediately behind them were the archers and three divisions of cavalry.

The Roman headquarters was now set up in front of the Psephinus tower. From this vantage point Titus could see the whole of his army and direct operations. He was going to launch a major assault. The officers were waiting for orders. Titus had chosen the northern wall for the first attack on Jerusalem. He left his tent so as to watch his men's movements. The war machines, several storeys high and filled with archers, slowly rolled towards the wall. The battering-rams went into operation. Each man was well instructed, well disciplined and knew exactly how to handle these efficient war machines which, through a system of winches, counterweights and balance wheels, were able to catapult stones—all weighing over 100 lb—more than three hundred yards.

The wall was assailed simultaneously from three sides by a powerful burst of fire from the machines. The alert was sounded. The fighting men formed up and John of Gischala arrived to take stock of the situation. 'Five hundred determined men can destroy Titus' machine. They can go through the rear gate near the Hippicus tower. The enemy will not see them.' Some time previously John had ordered a secret opening to be dug in the ramparts which would be masked by thick undergrowth. Without being noticed, the Jewish force descended unexpectedly on the Roman forces. There was furious hand-to-hand fighting. Fire swept the entrenchments and machines. Titus moved in in force, but it was too late. Despite enormous losses, the Jewish operation had succeeded.

Night fell. When there was silence once more, the men sat round on the ground and discussed the cause of the disaster. A centurion came up to one of the groups. 'It was only an accident,' he said. But the men did not believe him. 'It certainly wasn't an accident,' said one of them. 'There is something supernatural around us.' 'You're right,' said another one. 'This city isn't like anywhere else.' He got up and looked at Jerusalem with sparkling eyes. 'Sometimes I'm afraid in front of these walls, whereas at Jotapata or Gamala it made no difference to me. I don't know much about the sanctuary that's in there, in front of us, nor about the God the Jews worship...' He turned towards his friends. 'But haven't you heard people say that unless we have wings none of us will be able to get inside this strange city?' The centurion smiled, shrugged his shoulders and went away muttering to himself, 'Stupid superstitions...' But he thought about what the young soldier had said for a long time afterwards.

*   *   *

On May 25, 70, Titus called a hundred men to install and move into position a new weapon that the Roman engineers had perfected and which had not yet been in operation. It was a powerful, complicated machine capable of firing a number of heavy lead balls all at the same time. The outer wall of Jerusalem received the impact of these huge missiles, along with three powerful battering-rams. The Jewish soldiers had to retreat. They were exhausted from fighting night and day, and lacked modern weapons. A large breach was made in the wall and the Romans poured into it.

Titus spoke to his general staff. 'In my view the Jews have just made a major tactical error. I have no idea whether they are at the end of their tether or victims of an error of judgement. Whatever the explanation, they have abandoned a wall which they could still have defended. No doubt they thought it preferable to abandon the outer wall so as to protect the other two better, but they are going to pay heavily for it. Even so, their resistance is astonishing. We ought not to conceal from ourselves the fact that our losses have been considerable in both men and material, and we have hardly reached the suburbs of the city. Of course we must attack and attack, but not waste lives.' From his position in the place of the Assyrians, Titus prepared in great detail the assault on the second wall which protected the new town.

John of Gischala regarded the situation as serious, and personally took in hand the direction of operations from the Antonia tower. Simon ben Giora had drawn up his forces not far from John Hyrcanus' monument. They made several assaults in an attempt to stave off the attack, but the Jews lacked tactical experience and in the close fighting were more often the underdogs. However, these reverses did not break the extraordinary spirit of the men. Simon ben Giora was a strong and charismatic leader and his troops obeyed him unquestioningly. He led the most desperate actions personally, and stayed with his troops to the very end.

Another attack began. Night and day Jews and Romans were locked in extremely violent conflict. Titus had brought together more than ten thousand picked troops. After some days the wall was breached and the Romans entered the town in large numbers. They moved among the stalls that were still loaded with woollens, clothing and scrap-iron.

Titus imagined that he could demoralize both the fighting men and the population by announcing through heralds that houses would not be burned, prisoners would be well treated, and that pillaging would be punished by death. John and Simon consulted together and replied with a public declaration stating that whoever spoke of capitulation and defeatism would be severely punished.

The Jewish defenders knew all the twisting alleys of the district which had just been invaded. Hardly had the Romans ventured into them than they were welcomed by a hail of missiles. A battle began, street by street and house by house. Jewish fighters lay in wait in obscure corners and struck down lone Roman soldiers who had lost their way and were going round in circles in the tortuous maze. Arrows were fired from rooftops and windows. The Romans, walking along blindly, were terrified, and tried to take refuge in the houses. They broke down doors with their feet but the Jewish fighters inside either stabbed them or murdered them.

The massacre took on such horrifying proportions that the Roman command ordered the men back. The survivors regrouped, abandoned their dead and injured in the trap they had walked into, and went back through the wall.

Victory was announced in the Jewish camp, but the respite was short-lived. Titus took the failure as a personal insult. He ordered in fresh troops and gained the offensive. Three days later the Romans took the second wall once more, and did not let go again.

*   *   *

Roman pressure was becoming intense, and Jerusalem was suffering. Family food stocks were rapidly being exhausted. Bread made from wheat flour—the bread of the rich—had long since disappeared. Bread made from barley was becoming rare. The usual vegetables of the citizens— beans, lentils, cucumbers and onions—were sold in pitiful quantities. There was not even any salsify on the shelves. As for fish, the sea and the Lake of Tiberias were a long way off.

The black market appeared and prices accelerated madly. Barter came into daily life. The rich exchanged their goods for a sack of wheat, the poor for a handful of barley. The housewives were worn out through fruitless journeys to market, and complained about the people who feathered their own nests and had monopolies. Public distribution of food did not appease the bitterness, especially since the rations grew smaller each day. On the surface, morale remained firm, but concern unconsciously turned into anxiety. Roman agents infiltrated the town, choosing the most propitious places, such as shops and markets, to spread their defeatist talk.

On June 4, 70 the blows of the battering rams suddenly stopped. A heavy silence settled over Jerusalem. All at once, groups of men and women went towards the ramparts. The procession grew, and soon a vast throng, leaning through the battlements, was watching the Roman camp. The ceremony mounted by Titus for the benefit of the besieged was just beginning. The whole army was drawn up in front of the emperor's son to receive its pay and its rewards. All the men were armed from head to foot, their swords drawn and their breastplates sparkling. Hundreds of chariots, collapsing beneath the weight of the food they carried, arrived in the camp from around Jerusalem. A massive distribution of food lasted four days. Under the eyes of the starving people, joking soldiers unloaded meat and dried fish, vegetables and fruit, and goatskins full of the thick, heavy wine of Galilee. Without a movement the Jewish people clenched their fists. There was not a cry or a curse.

Titus did not give up, but a week went by and there was no sign of any unbending on the part of the people defending the city. The interruption of the siege and his exercise in propaganda had been rewarded with failure. He sent for Josephus. 'Go and speak to them. Tell them that they are already beaten though they don't realize it. Tell these madmen that I am offering them an honourable peace if they stop the fighting.' Like a prowler Josephus slowly went up to the wall, taking care to remain out of reach of any arrows. 'The strongest of your walls have been knocked down. The one that remains is weaker than the ones that have fallen.' He was interrupted by screams. Insults burst out. He turned pale and tried to continue. 'Throw away your weapons, have pity on your country...' Stones followed insults, then arrows and burning brands. Josephus retreated, and on the ramparts there was derision.

Inside the city there was no longer poverty, but famine. People were afraid of their neighbours. They hid their meagre provisions in the most secret corners of their living quarters. Doors were left open because a closed-up house became suspect. It was believed that people hid so as to eat in secret. At night both men and women went as far as the first Roman entrenchments to dig up a few mouldy vegetables or wild herbs. They were lucky if, on the way back, other starving people did not take this pitiful booty from them.

The defenders of the Antonia fortress had repelled all the attacks, but now there was a new threat. From their command post John of Gischala and Simon ben Giora noticed with concern the terracing that the Romans had constructed at the foot of the east wall. John gave the order for shafts to be sunk under the terracing, and for these to be filled with combustible material. The best sappers set to work at once. When the underground passages were ready a soldier set light to the dry wood and tar that had been stacked up there. There was almost a volcanic eruption. The earth rose up in a whirlwind of dust. Flames sprang up and spread to the siege machines. The Antonia was saved.

Titus was speaking to his general staff whom he had summoned urgently. 'Our lines are too weak. Our patrols are not sufficient to stop people getting into Jerusalem.' The meeting promised to be a heated one, because the officers were in disagreement on the strategy to be adopted. Some maintained that only an all-out attack would put an end to Jewish resistance. Others maintained that the terracing ought to be rebuilt, and above all that there should be an increase in the watch on the ways out of the city through which some convoys of food were still slipping. Titus hesitated, then opted for the blockade. A wall nearly five miles long was to be built round Jerusalem to prevent any mass exodus and any food going in. Titius' goal was to ensure total famine.

Jerusalem was now cut off from the world and horror was visible all around. Life was suspended. Passers-by kept close to the wall as they went silently about the city, their complexions pale, their faces swollen. In the suffocating alleys pestilential odours hung heavily. Bodies lay on the paving stones, next to mountains of rubbish where furtive people would occasionally come, to scavenge feverishly. On the terrace rooftops women and children in a state of exhaustion seemed to wait for death. Minds became hardened and lost sensitivity. The mortality rate was so high that no one bothered with sepulchres any more. Houses which had been abandoned by their owners were stacked with corpses and the entries and exits blocked up. Otherwise the corpses were thrown into ravines where they were inextricably mixed with each other. When there was an organized sally, the troops had to cross this monstrous piling up of decomposing corpses before they could throw themselves on the enemy.

As the famine got worse, the number of people who fled increased. When they reached the Roman camp they had not eaten for so long and threw themselves so voraciously on the food they were given that they immediately died because their bodies were so unused to normal functions. One day a refugee, who was little more than a skeleton, was found near an Arab garrison examining his own excrement. Before leaving the city the man had swallowed some pieces of gold and was trying to find them. The mercenary soldiers who captured him put the word around that all the refugees had stomachs full of gold. The hunt was on. Hundreds of Jews were taken and pitilessly disembowled. When Titus was informed of the practice the mercenaries were indulging in, he was beside himself. He called the leaders of the auxiliary troops to him. 'Your men, who have the honour of fighting under my orders, are making the name of Rome vile. Are you not ashamed? Arabs and Syrians may behave as they wish when they fight elsewhere, but I will not tolerate that they make the Romans share their cruelty and their hatred for the Jews. Anyone who commits a similar crime again will be put to death.'

*   *   *

By July 20, only the Antonia fortress protected the sanctuary against the fury of Rome. It was a vast cube flanked by four towers and placed on a naked rock. Inside were living quarters, armouries and even banqueting rooms and baths. Outside, smooth polished walls made any attempt at scaling it very difficult.

After the first attack one of the towers collapsed, but the amazed Romans were confronted by an enormous rampart which had been rapidly built by John of Gischala's men. Doubt and a sense of discouragement overtook the Roman cohorts, to the extent that Titus intervened personally to rally them. 'If you take the fortress, the whole city is yours.' The general assault was launched in the middle of the night. The Jews knew that the Temple was the stake in the struggle, and showed incredible courage. The fighting was so close that the men were unable to use arrows or spears on either side. Intense hand-to-hand fighting lasted until the morning, and the outcome was undecided. The massacre was so great that Titus was contented with the ground he had gained and put off until later the attack on the Temple.

*   *   *

Jerusalem was disintegrating. Members of the same family fought each other ferociously for scraps of food. People began to suspect the dying of pretending to be in the last throes so as to get a few grains of wheat. Corpselike figures with swollen stomachs collapsed in the middle of the

street after staggering around for hours. Everything was devoured: scraps
of hay, pieces of belts or sandals, skin from the shields.

Two soldiers were walking in a deserted alley in Jerusalem. Suddenly they were aware of a smell of cooked meat coming from a house.
They broke down the door and found a woman squatting in a corner. One
of the soldiers shouted at her: 'We'll kill you unless you show us what
you are eating.'

'I've kept a good helping for you,' she said. and the unfortunate
woman offered to the horrified soldiers the remains of her own child.

'Eat it,' the woman screamed. 'I've had some, too. Surely you are no
weaker than a woman or more pitiable than a mother.' She laughed
viciously. 'If you are pious and don't want any, then I've tasted some for
you. Leave the rest to me.'

This crime plunged Jerusalem into shame and terror. Traitors
hastened to spread false rumours:

'Take care. This is not an isolated incident. There are bands of can-
nibals everywhere, stalking their prey.' The people were swept by fear.
Parents forbade their children to go out alone.

There was an outburst against the Jews among the Romans.

'I told you so,' said an officer to his friends. 'They are monsters.
They're all monsters. Do you think that woman ate her child because she
was hungry? No. It's quite simply a human sacrifice. The Jews usually
eat the entrails of their victims. Fanatics and hypocrites, that's what they
are.'

'It's true,' added a centurion. 'I know them. I've seen them in Rome
and other places. Worship a universal God, do they? Then why do they
keep Him to themselves? We willingly welcome foreign religions, don't
we? Then why do they stop us going into their Temple? I've come to
think that they worship the head of an ass.'

'A pig more like. That's probably why they don't want to eat any
of it.'

One morning thousands of faithful Jews went up to the Temple for
the daily service. They were asked to go home. Sacrifice had ceased
because there was nothing to offer God.

Titus wanted to put an end to it. The House of the Word and the
Scripture was still standing insolently on Mount Moriah. The Roman

soldiers were working feverishly to build new terracing at the north-west angle of the Temple and at the west gate.

John and Simon were strongly entrenched. They held the first spurs of the hill and still had war machines on the great platform. Their communications were not threatened, and John could easily reach Simon by a footbrige joining the royal palace to some of the temple galleries. They were awaiting a new assault.

In the middle of the night a band of Roman troops attacked the Temple guard but did not succeed in defeating them. Then John of Gischala launched a distracting operation against some of the Roman entrenchments surrounding Jerusalem, but there was a strong counter-offensive, which forced the Jewish troops to fall back on Mount Moriah, where they tirelessly repelled Roman attacks day after day.

One morning a unit pretended to abandon one part of the wall. The ruse worked. The Romans drew up their machines, climbed the rampart and attacked the portico. But a fierce fire broke out at their feet. The scaffolding collapsed, dragging the soldiers with it. Those who were left clinging to the portico and escaped the flames were killed with spears.

*   *   *

John and Simon continued the struggle. The Jews were implacable. Titus thought that it was high time to decide the fate of the Temple, but he hesitated to take alone a decision that was so heavy with consequences. He called together his six leading commanders. Each one of them knew Titus wanted to save the Temple. But they all hoped to make him change his mind. The meeting began and the senior general allowed his officers to speak quite freely. The temperature went up immediately. One general expostulated:

'The Jews forced this war on us. We should bring the rules of war into operation. John and Simon have turned the Temple into a fortress. Is it still a sanctuary? No. It is nothing more than a military objective like the others. An objective to be achieved.'

'But we should not take such a decision quickly,' counted Tiberius Alexander. 'Let the Jews be told that if they evacuate the Temple and take all their weapons away, we are prepared to spare it. If they persist, then they carry the blame for its destruction.'

Marcus Julianus spoke next:

'Remember that the Temple is the supreme symbol of the religion and the nation, the place of assembly of all the Jews throughout the world. If it remains standing, we shall only have won a false victory. Revolt will continue to simmer, then explode one day or another, once again. Have you forgotten that of all the people we have defeated, the Jews are the only ones to have risen against Rome?'

Titus spoke. He had listened to and taken note of all the arguments.

'I reject the idea of taking revenge on a building for the crimes committed by men. I think, in the last resort, that Rome's prestige has everything to gain by safeguarding so famous a monument.'

The meeting was over. Titus had decided. He got up and left.

The commanders looked at each other, exchanged a few words and shrugged their shoulders. Marcus Julianus took Tiberius Alexander by the arm and led him into a corner of the tent.

'Taking revenge on a building ... So famous a monument ... Do you really think that Titus believes in this nonsense?'

'What do you mean?'

'Didn't you notice that at one point in the discussion Titus remained silent for a long time, looking vague. I'm sure he was thinking about Berenice and the promise he once made to her to save the sanctuary of the Jews. That princess is a clever woman. Her caprice could cause all our projects to fail, and spoil our triumph.'

The officers parted. Regardless of whether they were satisfied they would obey.

*   *   *

For six days on end, without pause, the battering-rams attacked the last rampart, while the Romans dug tunnels under the foundations of the north gate. The attackers tried the impossible. They put their ladders against the porticos and began to climb, with their shields above their heads. Hardly had they reached the top than they were pushed and knocked into space. A Jew got hold of a Roman standard and waved it triumphantly. But with a deafening growl reinforcements of cavalry and infantry rushed on to the Temple platform. The waves of assault became more violent and more murderous. Overwhelmed by exhaustion, hunger and the dreadful heat, the Jews retreated to the sanctuary so as to avoid being surrounded.

On August 29, 70 a golden window on the north side of the Temple was undefended. Slowly a Roman soldier left the scene of the battle and went towards the wall. He called a colleague, climbed on to the other's shoulders, looked around, and threw his torch. The fire did not begin at once, but within minutes gained ground. When the smoke began to billow the Roman soldiers gave a great shout of joy.

A breathless messenger startled Titus, asleep in his tent. 'Lord, someone has set fire to the Temple.' Titus sat up, went pale, then jumped from his camp bed, gathered a group of officers and hurried towards Mount Moriah. He found an incoherent tumult. 'Put out the fire. Put out the fire.' Titus yelled his orders. He shouted and threatened, to no avail. The soldiers continued to advance with their firebrands in their hands. Their shouts swamped Titus' voice and his orders. In solid masses the Romans, Arabs and Syrians rushed to the Temple walls and almost as if they regretted not having been able to start the fire, vied with one another for the glory of throwing their flaming brands into the flames.

As the fire reached the buildings, large numbers of famished and unarmed citizens of Jerusalem or pilgrims massed together on the terraces and in the courts. Uncontrolled soldiers massacred them pitilessly and rolled their bodies down the staircases. The corpses fell to the ground on top of one another, not far from where a group of priests, surrounded by flames, stretched out their arms and recited prophetic verses or pronounced anathemas against Titus and Rome.

The officers were nauseated and gave up attempting to re-establish order in their ranks. The soldiers became pillaging hordes. Kicking corpses aside, they rushed towards God's House before fire prevented access. The gold and silver decorations were torn down, sacred vessels, embroidered fabrics and strips of the great Babylonian curtain were passed from hand to hand. Bursts of laughter and shouts covered the noise of falling beams. The altar was split by axes and the seven-branched candelabrum dragged from the Temple.

In the cellars where the treasury rooms were situated the soldiers plunged their arms to the bottom of the coffers and poured into sacks thousands of gold and silver pieces, medals and rare coins. They carried off the trophies and the ornaments and quarrelled fiercely over the precious objects.

While his legions indulged in their murderous madness, Titus, accompanied by his lieutenants, went into the Holy of Holies, which had not yet been touched by the fire. He was anxious, as Pompey had been a hundred and thirty-three years before. The small square room was void —a dizzy void.

Titus left the Holy of Holies, troubled by the first clouds of smoke. The fire had not increased. Possibly there was still time to save the Temple. He threw himself in front of his soldiers, and once more urged them to put out the fire. He called to a centurion: 'Copy me. Order your men to put out the fire. Strike the ones who refuse to obey you. That's an order.' The centurion jumped on his soldiers and shouted the general's orders. He was greeted with only jeers. In an act of defiance a frenzied soldier rushed towards one of the doors, slid in a burning brand and rushed away. The fire now raced across the interior of the Temple.

John and Simon succeeded in penetrating the Roman lines. They took refuge in the upper town and regrouped what was left of their forces. The Temple was on fire but Jerusalem had not been taken.

Within the holy precinct, where fighting had stopped, the sound of trumpets rang out. Centurions solemnly carried the emblems of the legions and placed them opposite the west door. The Romans shouted '*Titus imperator*! *Titus imperator*!' Titus stood and savoured his victory. He was already thinking about the triumph his father was storing up for him in Rome.

He looked towards the top of a wall. Silent priests, pale and starved, had just witnessed the sacrifices that the Romans had offered to their gods at the very heart of a profaned Jerusalem. The ceremony was over. Titus called a centurion. 'Make the priests come down.' Held up by soldiers, the dying men went slowly towards the general, who was waiting for them with a smile on his lips. 'No doubt you are going to ask me to spare your lives. I would gladly have pardoned you if your Temple had not been destroyed. But now I presume that life no longer has any meaning for you. Isn't it proper for the priests to disappear with their sanctuary?'

Titus made a sign to his guards. The priests were led outside the court. An hour later they were savagely executed after being torn by whips.

*   *   *

John and Simon had replied with contempt to Josephus' last exhortation to surrender. They did not want any discussion with the renegade Jew, but nevertheless agreed to hear directly the intentions of the Roman command. If Titus was intransigent, if he demanded a dishonourable surrender, talks would be broken off. A meeting was fixed for the following day.

Titus and his retinue walked slowly on to the bridge which joined the Temple platform to Mount Zion. At the other end of the bridge John of Gischala and Simon ben Giora, with armed men, walked towards Titus. The two processions stopped in front of each other. Titus spoke first:

'Before the outbreak of war I warned you against the use of force. You didn't listen to me. Although my men wanted to exterminate you, I restrained them. After each of my army's victories I renewed my efforts for peace. But it was useless. When I reached Mount Moriah I refused to put into operation the rules of war, and I begged you to spare both the sacred vessels and your Temple. You are responsible for these massacres and these ruins. And now here you are before me, still armed, as if you were not beaten. Give yourselves up, and your lives will be spared.'

After a long silence John of Gischala's voice was heard.

'We have sworn never to give up. We will stand by our oath. Let us leave Jerusalem with our women and children and the city is yours.'

Titus turned pale.

'Your people are annihilated, your fathers' sanctuary in ruins, and you dare dictate conditions to me! If you still have any strength left, carry on the fight. I would be ashamed to accept even a minor compromise.'

The guerrilla warfare started up again. Four legions had taken up their position in front of the walls near the royal palace, building terraces and bringing up new siege machines.

The disproportion in the forces was now overwhelming. The Roman troops were well-fed and in high spirits because of their victories. The Jews were disheartened and weak from hunger. When the battering-rams attacked the rampart and the Romans got ready for the assault, hundreds of Jewish fighters gave up and hid in the countless underground passages below Jerusalem. Only the most fanatic troops tried to stop the inexorable Roman advance, but they could only offer pitiful rear-guard actions.

Some of the towers were still intact, and John and Simon thought about occupying them with the last of their troops. Simon inspected them very carefully, in the utmost secrecy, but he realized that it would be impossible to carry on any resistance there for more than a few days, because of the total lack of food. The two men then felt themselves driven to supreme decisions. They knew that Titus had sent out special agents and contingents to hunt them down. They became obsessed with the idea of escaping the enemy. The country was broken, occupied and terrorized, but they owed it to themselves to remain available for the future struggles which Roman oppression would make inevitable. John and Simon rallied their followers. 'If we can get through Titus' wall we shall be free.' The little band went down into the Valley of Kedron and began to climb the wall. A Roman sentry saw them and gave the alert. Roman soldiers flooded the spot in compact masses, blocked the way and threw them back in disorder.

John succeeded in getting back to Jerusalem. Impatient to escape, he told a friend who was hiding him that he was going to try to get out through the sewers. 'This time I have every chance of getting through; now that the fighting has fallen off, they are bound to be less watchful.' One night, as darkness fell, John and three companions climbed down into an underground passage that was to take them out of the city. After walking for an hour they became anxious, for the darkness was as thick as ever and the endless passage did not seem to lead anywhere. They retraced their steps in search of a way out, but to no avail. Anxiety took hold of them. They turned into a side passage, but it led nowhere. Then they tried to go back to where they had come from, lost their way and went round in circles. Suddenly a terrible smell gripped them. In the dark they had walked into a pile of corpses which had been thrown hurriedly into a conduit. Horrified, the men struck out in another direction. Time passed. They began to be exhausted. After a few hours of restless sleep, the men began once more to make their way, as if in a trance, through the foul underground.

One man collapsed. 'I can't go on.' he groaned. 'Leave me and get away.' His comrade put him over his shoulder and the walk resumed. Suddenly John shouted 'Light!' They rushed towards a dimly lit opening at the end of the passage. John poked his head out and took a deep breath. They were in a little rural suburb of Jerusalem, beyond the walls. He turned round and signalled to his friends. The four of them emerged. John suggested that they separate and each try his luck. They embraced without a word, then John hurried off along a narrow twisting path between tall grass. When he reached the first houses of a village he proceeded carefully along a street and reached a little square. A Roman patrol was crossing; hesitating for only a second, he began to run. A centurion saw him and the patrol followed. The soldiers soon caught him, and then shouted in his face, 'You are John of Gischala.' No longer having the strength to defend himself, or to deny the accusation, John murmured, 'I can't go on. Give me a piece of bread.'

Roman guards walked round the blackened ruins of the Temple. Suddenly a man emerged from the mouth of a gutter. His arms were extended and he was dressed in a long white tunic and a purple cloak. The soldiers stopped short, taken aback, as they looked at the unbelievable figure. They could not move. After a few moments of amazement a centurion came forward slowly with his hand on his sword.

'Who are you?'

'I will tell only your leader. Call him immediately.'

The centurion turned on his heel and went off quickly. A commander appeared on the esplanade, went up to the man and shouted in turn:

'Who are you?'

The reply came at once: 'You have before you Simon ben Giora.' The officer refused to believe him. 'You are lying,' he yelled.

'I am telling the truth. I am Simon ben Giora.'

Two guards seized him, tied him up, dragged him off and threw him into a cell.

Simon's strategy had failed. In his delirium he had imagined he could terrorize the credulous and superstitious Roman soldiers by appearing before them suddenly on the very site of the Temple in a ghostly disguise, and then escape in the midst of the ensuing confusion.

*   *   *

'We fought with God. He alone could have driven the Jews out of this fortress.' Titus was walking around the centre of Jerusalem with his retinue. He walked the length of the fortifications and admired their enormous size. He was amazed at the towers and the dungeons, at their magnificence and the size of the blocks of stone.

He added: 'Without the help of God, my men and even my machines would never have come to the end of it.'

'Sir,' said an officer, 'do you know that behind the walls of these fortresses many victims of the Jewish leaders are still imprisoned?'

'What!' exclaimed Titus. 'I demand that they be set free at once, given food and comforted. They are doubtless good people who helped us in order to rid themselves of the tyranny of their leaders. Quickly, give the necessary orders.'

Throughout Jerusalem those who had survived the slaughter timidly reappeared from the sewers and cellars where they had hidden during the fighting. Dizzy from the light and open air, they ventured out into the streets, horrified by the sight of the ruins and the devastation. They spoke to each other softly and dispersed as soon as they caught sight of a Roman soldier. When Titus returned to his headquarters, he listened to the report of an officer who had just crossed the city to see where there might be pockets of resistance.

'Jerusalem is quiet, sir, but there is still quite a large population.'

'I consider all the inhabitants,' said Titus, 'as prisoners of war. Anyone who is armed or is hiding arms is to be executed, as for the others . . .'

Titus called one of his closest friends, Fronto, who was a loyal commandant, and ready to undertake any task.

'You know the problems. I leave it to you to decide the fate of the Jews of Jerusalem. In any case, we do not have enough wheat to feed them all.'

Day after day, in every district, there were huge round-ups brutally carried out by units of legionaries. Then a strict selection began, personally supervised by Fronto. Boys under seventeen were taken from their parents and brought to open ground near Jerusalem. Slave dealers indicated the boys that pleased them and sordidly bargained for the youths whom they purchased in lots of five and ten. They later sold them individually in countries near and far.

Young people over seventeen were put in chains and sent to Egypt for forced labour or put in reserve to appear in Titus' triumph. The circus in Caesarea, and elsewhere, also took its share of human flesh. Fronto inspected hundreds of men and chose the strongest and most handsome. They were to perish at the hands of the gladiators or be torn apart by wild beasts to the cheers of crowds eager for blood.

Below the gutted ramparts, in a huge camp, thousands of men and women, exhausted and abandoned to their fate, slowly died. Many of them refused all food when it came from Roman hands. They preferred to die of starvation.

*   *   *

From now on in the annihilated city the only noise that broke the silence was that of the passing Roman patrols. Men and women stumbled through the rubble of the demolished streets, searching in the ruins of their houses. Little groups formed on Mount Moriah. No one said a word. Each looked with tearful eyes at the esplanade which was now desolate but where, a thousand years ago, Solomon had built the first sanctuary of God. Fearing incidents, the soldiers came on the scene and cleared the site, pushing away the bravest, whose presence on the sacred spot seemed an intolerable act of defiance.

The bloody summer was over. In spite of the disaster and the dreadful loss of human life, Jerusalem retained an invincible hope. The Jews had known other calamities and their faith had never been extinguished. In their present misery the Jewish people vaguely obeyed one ideal: resistance to Rome. They had once resisted the insolence of Egypt, of Babylon, of Syria. They must not give up, but rather find new ways of carrying on the struggle.

Surrounded by his army, Titus departed from Jerusalem, leaving only the Tenth Legion and a few squadrons of cavalry to keep order. Titus crossed the ramparts and took the road for the sea. He was overcome with loneliness and anxiety. He knew that in Caesarea Berenice was waiting for him. He would be greeted as a liar. He wondered whether he, Titus, a Roman General, should admit that he had never imagined such an implacable resistance, that he had only been able to answer fury with fury? Somehow he would try to persuade her that the efforts to save the Temple had been in vain. Night had fallen long since, and Titus could see no more of Jerusalem than a black line darkening the horizon. The pale reflection of the night lit the shadow of the ruins of the Holy City with an opaque light. As Titus moved further away from the site of his victory, Jerusalem seemed to him to be drowned more and more in strange shadows. But Jerusalem, given up in time of defeat, flattened under dislodged stones, gradually, imperceptibly, began to move under the effect of a spiritless life. The broken blocks which littered the site of the desolate sanctuary suddenly aligned themselves geometrically and found once more, in the darkness, the order that the God of Lightness wanted. Jerusalem formed again out of herself, and no one was there to see that the city was indestructible.

The forgotten dead, the martyr priests and the avenging soldiers inhabited this apocalyptic universe. Meanwhile the Roman garrison left by Titus to watch over their portion of nothingness, prudently withdrew to the surrounding heights, and set up its camp on the edge of the chasm of man's memory.

6 Israel without the Temple

'Master, it is time to say the morning prayer.' Rabbi Johanan ben Zakkai slowly tore himself away from the text he had been studying since midnight. 'Is the East ablaze?' he asked his disciples, and without waiting for a reply got up and began to recite the *Shema*: 'Hear, O Israel, the Lord our God, the Lord is one.'

During the night some young Pharisees had arrived in Yabne. They had wandered for several months around the ruins of Jerusalem, rather as an eagle which does not want to believe that its nest has been robbed hovers in the air. But finally they decided to join the man who, before the last fatal battle, had left the Holy City to open a school. The new arrivals had long been tempted to join the surviving Zealots who had taken refuge in Masada, and to carry on the struggle as if the Temple had not been burned. But out of Johanan ben Zakkai and Eleasar ben Yair, these Pharisees chose the person who renounced killing, bloodshed, and suicide, in an attempt to lift the independence of Israel to an impregnable and unassailable summit, represented by the Torah, the preservation of which lay in study.

Morning prayer rose up from every part of Yabne. Rabbi Johanan's disciples recited both to themselves and together, the verses of the Torah which enjoined the love of the personal and unique God, and the love of one's neighbour. There were no distinctions between the pupils of the school at Yabne. There were no more practising priests and no more Levites. Masters and pupils were indistinguishable. It was not yet a year since the Holy of Holies had gone up in smoke, and these men gave no sign of mourning the great catastrophe. They knew that they were forming a new bond that would join them—this time in an irrevocable way—to the all-powerful Lord.

Prayers were over. Everyone went towards the hall of the academy, where the master of Yabne was to give his lecture. They all listened to him and then went off in little groups to recapitulate the contents of the day's lesson. Each one deliberately put questions to himself and to his colleagues, and each person attempted to reply. For an hour the master had talked, teaching that the best thing for man is contentment and the worst, discontent. It is better to bring others to do good than to do it oneself. Even if there had been only one just man, it would have been worth creating the world. Charity is rewarded to the extent of the goodness inherent in it. The man who does his charitable deeds in secret has more influence with God than Moses himself.

One of the men arrived late and heard Rabbi Johanan speak for the first time, had the audacity to interrupt him. 'Master, how can we obtain God's forgiveness when the Temple has been burned down and the expiatory sacrifices are no longer possible?'

Rabbi Johanan answered with three sentences:

'Prayer is better than sacrifice. Charity is better than all sacrifices. Justice raises up a nation and charity serves as expiatory sacrifice for Israel and the other nations.'

Everyone now realized that Rabbi Johanan did not expect that the Temple would be rebuilt in the near future.

In the days which followed, Johanan's pupils asked themselves what the significance of their master's latest teaching was. There were some for whom the battle of Jerusalem was still a vivid memory which continued to obsess them, and there were some who daily felt tempted to go and join the fighters at Masada. These people wondered whether the head of the school of Yabne meant that the Jewish nation was now no more than a dream, and that the independence of Israel had no importance in relation to the Divine project for Israel. There were many who thought, and said openly—convinced that they were the genuine interpreters of Rabbi Johanan's words—that since the Temple had been burned down, and sacrifice in the material sense was no longer possible, Judaism should carry on in another form.

Others maintained that if Israel abandoned its nationality it would cease to exist. Despite the destruction of the Temple, and the fact that Israel was unable to sacrifice to its God, independence was the guarantee of the survival of the Jewish people. Therefore the Temple had to be rebuilt, as quickly as possible, to facilitate the Messiah's arrival. After all, for more than two centuries the Jewish people had fought continually in order to make possible the triumphant arrival of the Saviour.

Fragments of these discussions got back to Rabbi Johanan. The whole of his teaching—of which he had inspired and illuminated knowledge—was obviously aimed at ensuring the permanence of Israel's existence.

*   *   *

Rabbi Johanan had realized before most others that the Temple would be destroyed, that Roman oppression would get worse, and that any new attempt at revolt would be a bloodbath. He knew that the motive force of revolution had always been the announcement of the advent of the Messiah. The people only rose up to fight the occupying power when they thought that God's envoy was in their midst, or at the very least that his advent was imminent. It would seem then that in order to have the peace necessary for the re-establishing of Jewish existence, the people would have to be separated from Messianic expectation. But that was impossible. Rabbi Johanan merely taught that the arrival of the Messiah was absolutely unforeseeable. No one could say when, or in what circumstances, he would come.

Rabbi Johanan may well have been disturbed by the activities of the earliest followers of Jesus of Nazareth, who—in order to attract converts—exploited the announcement the Jews made of the imminent arrival of the Messiah. His teaching about the Messiah was doubtless influenced accordingly, but the fundamental reason was without a doubt his wish to prevent this belief from dragging the people into more revolts, more death, and more collective suicide.

All the students at Yabne realized that the voice from Heaven could only be that of the Messiah at the end of the world. Rabbi Johanan taught that the Jews should not hasten the end, since the Messiah could as easily come in a totally bad time as in a totally good one. One ought not risk adding to the evil, even in the interests of bringing closer the moment of salvation. Rabbi Johanan taught and his disciples repeated, 'The Son of David will not come until the Jews have despaired of redemption.'

Rabbi Johanan believed in the universal and totally pacifist ideal of the Pharisees, and took pains to remind his disciples that the God of the Jews was the king of the whole earth, and that the aim of creation was to bring the age of peace when 'They shall beat their swords into plowshares, and their spears into pruninghooks.' He therefore taught that they should prevent towns from being fortified. He required rigid and unconditional application of the commandments of the Torah from his pupils, with the obvious exception of those laws governing the Temple worship.

But he believed that translation of the Jewish holy books would be dangerous because of those who denounced the faith. He was also aware of the
fact that as the fame of his school spread it would attract many to Yabne
who were lost without the Temple. He therefore allowed some of the
Temple liturgy to be introduced at Yabne, but all the same it was not
Jerusalem—even though large crowds arrived on the feasts of
pilgrimage.

Rabbi Johanan had now put the Jews on the right path. He was
convinced of the fact, as were his disciples. But he suffered the fate of
all reformers. He had to leave the place so as to allow his successors to
assure the continuity of the tradition he had begun. One day, when he had
given his lesson, he turned towards Gamaliel, his oldest associate and the
son of Simon ben Gamaliel, one of the leaders of the council of Jerusalem
during the revolt against Rome. Slowly Johanan invested Gamaliel who
immediately began his teaching while Johanan himself set off towards the
little village of Beyrur Ha'il, where he began his lessons for other disciples.
On his deathbed, Johanan had still one more lesson for his pupils. When
they heard that he was ill, all the faithful disciples of Yabne rushed to
Beyrur Ha'il.

Johanan wept.

'Light of Israel, pillar of justice, strong hammer, why are you weeping? Johanan replied: 'I would weep if someone were to take me before
a king of flesh and blood who today lives but tomorrow might be resting
in his grave; whose anger is not an eternal anger; whose prison is not
an eternal prison; whose condemnation to death would not send me to
an everlasting death; before a king whom I might influence by my words
or corrupt with money. I would not weep when they were going to take me
before the King of Kings, the Holy One, blessed be He, the Living One,
the Eternal, whose wrath, if it touched me, would last for ever; whose
prison, if I were shut up in it, would shut me up for ever; whose judgement, if the death sentence were pronounced on me, would strike me down
for ever; before the King who would not be influenced by my words or
corrupted by my money. But now there are two possible ways before me,
the Garden of Eden and the Valley of Hinnom, but I do not know which
of the two I shall be obliged to take.'

'Give us your blessing,' replied his disciples.

'Would that you feared Heaven as you fear a simple mortal.'

'No more?'

'Surely, do you not know that man, when he commits a sin, says "as long as no one sees me"?' (*Talmud*, Berahot 28b.) And Rabbi Johanan died.

*   *   *

'Master of the world, the hour of triumph has sounded.' Vespasian was awoken by his officers. Today he was to receive the sacred homage of the Roman people. Well before dawn the crowds had lined the Appian Way. They were all happy, and with good reason. The Jews who had rebelled had been reduced to a state of slavery. The civil war which had set Roman against Roman so cruelly was now over. Vespasian had been able to assert his rule and Rome carried on.

The Senate had set aside this day for the triumph of the conquerors of Judaea. The original supreme assembly of Rome had decided that Vespasian and Titus would each have his own triumph, so great were their individual merits. But out of affection for one another, Vespasian and Titus had decided that they would have only one triumph for one victory, which marked the success of a single family: the Flavians.

Vespasian and Titus left the Temple of Isis where they had spent the night; they were crowned with laurels and dressed in purple. They carried no arms. The Senate, the established institutions, and the great officials of the Empire were there waiting for them. When they arrived everyone saluted them. Then the speeches began. Each orator talked about the great military prowess of the emperor and his brave son, mentioning the glorious episodes and the movements of the war in Judaea.

Vespasian was first and foremost a soldier. He did not like big speeches. He stopped the speakers and the ceremony resumed. He covered his face with a fold of his toga and said the prayers and vows, thanking the gods for having brought him as far as this moment of triumph. Then all went in procession towards the celebrations which had been prepared at the triumphal arch. They ate, then offered sacrifices to the gods represented on the triumphal arch. There was Jupiter, the god of the gods, and Augustus, first Emperor of Rome, and above all Mars, the god of war. Vespasian and Titus were now wearing their ceremonial dress, and the parade began. The crowd was so great that there was just room for the procession to get by. Everyone wanted to touch the victors and spit on the defeated, admire the trophies, and the foreign gods that had been captured and brought to Rome.

Vespasian and Titus took their places on richly carved ivory chairs. Domitian, Vespasian's second son, joined them. The procession began.

First came all sorts of exotic animals unknown in Rome, then prisoners—
in chains, but wearing their national costumes, which gave them an
almost frivolous appearance, despite the stigmata of slavery they bore on
their bodies and in their faces. At the front of the column of prisoners were
Simon ben Giora and John of Gischala, proud and unbroken. The procession continued with floats several storeys high representing the
provinces of Judaea and the main towns at the time of the battle. At last
came the treasures from the Temple of Jerusalem.

Soldiers of Herculean proportions carried the monumental seven-
branched candelabrum made of solid gold and weighing more than a ton.
At the end of each branch was a lamp. The ensemble was richly sculpted
and represented the seven days of the week. Then came the altar of the
shewbread, also made of gold, and of considerable weight. Finally four
soldiers carried the magnificent curtain which concealed the Holy of
Holies. The people scarcely noticed the huge boxes full of gold pieces and
precious jewels.

Admiration was at its height and the crowd gave shouts of satisfaction. But when the victorious general, now Emperor of Rome, appeared,
enthusiasm was boundless. Vespasian was mounted on a marvellous white
horse, decked out in cloth that was sumptuously embroidered in silver.
The emperor sat very straight, and waved to the crowd. The ground in
front of him was spread with sweetly smelling flowers. Titus and Domitian
followed him respectfully. They received endless ovations from the youth
of Rome, full of romanticism and love of adventure. No one noticed the
black slave between Vespasian and his sons who continually whispered
mysterious words in Vespasian's ear. Only a few of the onlookers knew
that each person enjoying a triumph had to undergo this sad ritual, and
that the slave was saying to Vespasian the traditional words, 'Remember
that you are only a man.'

Popular excitement reached its zenith when the procession arrived at
the Temple of Capitoline Jupiter. Everyone stopped. There were a few
prayers, then Simon ben Giora was led to the steps of the temple, where
the executioner's axe descended, severing his life. The procession set off
again, finally to disperse.

*   *   *

Emperor Hadrian, who ascended the throne in 117, had been made wary
by the difficulties the Jews had created for his adoptive father, Trajan, and

took measures to diminish the vitality of Judaism. He began by forbidding circumcision. Then to avoid any resurgence of nationalist fervour, he forbade Jewish access to Jerusalem, with the exception of one day in the year, the 9th of Ab, the anniversary of the destruction of the Temple. Judaea lost its name and became Palestine, in memory of the Philistines who occupied the coastal strip when Joshua entered the Promised Land.

Hadrian knew all the same that these measures did not affect the new activity of the Jews: study. He was wary of these assemblies in which the people whom Vespasian had defeated pretended to deepen their religion. It was a study of revolt which presented the Romans as the enemy to be struck down. Hadrian therefore decided to forbid study meetings In this way he began a policy of total annihilation of the Jews, a policy of enforced assimilation to the Graeco-Roman ideal.

7 The Last Gasps

In the year 72, Samuel ben Ezra, his wife and their two children—a boy and a girl—arrived at Ein Gedi. They had fled Jerusalem as it was burning, determined to carry on the fight somewhere else and in another way. Samuel felt himself called by Masada, the old fortress restored by Herod. In spite of his impatience and keen desire to join the Jewish resistance, he had been forced to stop at Ein Gedi, an oasis by the Dead Sea, for his children were exhausted by the surreptitious way in which they had been obliged to travel since they had beaten the Roman blockade. Left behind and in flames were their few belongings and their little house in the lower town.

There was a short stream which ran into the Dead Sea, falling over the last obstacles in a series of waterfalls which in places made it look like a mountain torrent. Samuel and his wife spent a long time quenching their thirst while the children splashed about happily in this peaceful spot. Slowly, amidst the palm trees and the rank weeds, the images of death and destruction which haunted them, evaporated in the fading clearness of the sky.

Other refugees arrived, looking no more like fighters than Samuel did. They had no weapons and had the air of victims of this war rather than active participants in it. There was little conversation, but they soon knew that they all had a common aim, to get to Masada. Among the men present there was one held in a great respect. He was scarcely any older than the others, but he wore the tattered remnants of the garments the priests wore when they went about Jerusalem. His name was Simeon ben Yeozer. He said that at the time of Herod his father used to officiate and that on one occasion he had been to the palace fortress that the Idumean had had built at Masada. Herod had lived in perpetual fear of a Jewish revolt and had therefore wanted to build a stronghold that would be impregnable and in which, in case of danger, he might take refuge. But he feared the Egyptians as much as he feared the Jews, and the hold that the fiery Queen Cleopatra had over Antony, master of Rome. Cleopatra had wanted to push the borders of Egypt to Syria and have

Herod's head. So the Idumean had vast store-houses built at Masada, in which he began stocking immense amounts of food and arms. He had ordered his architects to build him a residence that would have all the comforts to which he was accustomed. There were Roman baths, terraces sheltered from the wind, and warm, spacious bedrooms.

But Simeon ben Yeozer said that the most extraordinary thing about Masada was the outer wall of the rock, which was highly fortified. It constituted an impregnable line of defence.

Samuel, thinking about his children, interrupted the priest and asked him how water supplies were obtained on a rocky height in the middle of the desert. Simeon replied that Herold had foreseen the problem, and immense cisterns had been sunk in non-porous ground. A network of canals collected every drop of rain, so that it was possible to grow vegetables at Masada. On the other hand, the priest added, the ground was so dry that food could be kept there indefinitely.

In spite of the risk of a Roman patrol coming on them, the men lit a fire. The women and children curled up at the bases of the trees and tried to sleep. The men listened far into the night to the man whose father had known Masada. There was no need to recall the recent history of the stronghold—how, at the start of the great revolt against Rome, Menahem and his Zealots captured it, taking the Roman garrison by surprise. And how Masada had been since then the nest of resistance to the Romans. When the angry people put Menahem to death, there was a return of patriots to the base, and since then they had been awaiting the confrontation with the Roman legions.

They had walked for five hours since dawn, and Masada rose out of the thin mist. The huge rock covered the deep depressions around it with its shadow. There were other peaks with more jagged outlines on the horizon, and they all looked impregnable, but Masada alone, because of its broad base, was unquestionably part of the ground. Nothing could shoulder aside this huge mass calmly placed on the earth out of which it had grown. Endless screes of stony blocks mixed with dusty yellow earth ran the length of the slopes, and the flattened summit deprived the rock of any natural character. Those beneath Masada felt that the life of man went on up there, that it was not an eagle's nest but, on the contrary, almost human architecture. Samuel and his family followed Simeon ben Yeozer, who pressed ahead. They wondered how to get to the top of such a mountain, under the midday sun. The motionless air which licked the banks of the Dead Sea did not awaken any atom of life in this transfixed universe. But for these men, Masada represented liberty, and possibly hope.

Instinctively, they now walked one behind the other. The route that they found on the east side of the fortress was not wide enough for two people to pass. The path was continually interrupted by huge rocks around which they had to make their way, so that every step forward seemed to take them further away from the goal. Progress was dangerous. Samuel and his wife had to help their children, because the risk of slipping on the dusty earth was great. For more than three hours they went on like this, overcome by heat and fatigue.

They were suddenly stopped by a sentry and asked why they had come to Masada. Without stopping, but lifting his head slightly with a tired look, Simeon replied: 'For the liberty of Jerusalem.' They were now only a little way from the top of the rock. They could see the outer wall, above which were enormous blocks of pink stone ready to be rolled down into the ravine. They went through the monumental entrance to the fortress which the defenders had always called the Gate of the Serpent Path. They noticed that the outer wall was in fact a double wall, and that there was enough space to live between the two sections of this line of defence.

They all sat down on the ground, utterly exhausted. The first, Simeon the priest, took note of things and ran his eye over the space where they would live. On his right he saw a long group of buildings upon which all the activity of the Zealots seemed to be concentrated. He guessed that they were the stores of food and arms. A soldier came out of one of the buildings, went towards the new arrivals and gave them dates, wheat, water, and to each man a sword, a bow and some arrows. The camp's command post must also be there.

As he ate, Simeon noticed three buildings on his left which he identified as the three little palaces that Herod had built in the centre of the fortress, the palaces seemingly secure from attacks. For the time being women and children brought almost happy activity to the place. The Zealots had turned the royal lodgings into billets. But just in front of them, at the other end of the esplanade, was a more stately palace which Herod had set aside for official ceremonies. Armed soldiers circled this palace which contained the throne room.

Simeon left the group of new arrivals and went towards the north part of the fortress where he knew there was a palace-villa that Herod had once had built as a place of rest. When he had passed the stores and the royal baths he moved along the casemate wall, and by a narrow path sunk in the stone he came to the northern extremity of Masada. Beneath his feet three successive terraces reached to the edge of the precipice. On the topmost was a massive building literally clinging to the rock. This palace ended in a semicircular porch overhanging the second terrace, with a circular pavillion surrounded by pink stone colonnades. The lowest esplanade had no buildings, but a series of columns with no practical purpose marked its limits. Before rejoining his travelling companions, Simeon noticed the mosaics covering the ground. On the return journey he encountered several groups of busy women and children.

The people he had just left had now formed a ring round a tall, spare man whose silhouette made a curious outline against the fading light of day. The man said that he was Eleazar ben Ya'ir, leader of Zealot resistance. He said that Masada was the base from which many expeditions set out against the Roman occupants, and that the nine hundred and sixty men, women and children living there had an impregnable place of refuge, as much through their determination for vengeance as through the large supplies of food, water, arms and munitions in reserve. Eleazar concluded that as long as the Temple of Jerusalem remained a heap of ruins, the Jews would not be able to rest; that armed combat was a sacred obligation, and that God would give to His own the strength to conquer the great idolatrous power which reigned over the world.

Before leaving them, the leader gave his orders. For their first night in Masada they would all sleep in the billets in the centre of the fortress, but as from the following day the men would take their places in the casemates of the outer wall, while waiting for their first mission outside the fortress.

Before obeying, Simeon cast a glance at the plain, which now seemed to him to be part of another world. Under the rays of the sinking sun each valley seemed to lead directly into nothing, and the fields where they ended seemed curiously bare.

*   *   *

Flavius Silva had been in command of the Roman forces in Judaea for only a few days. People no longer dared call the emperor's representative in this country the Roman procurator, for since its defeat the country no longer seemed to exist. In Caesarea, which was traditionally a cross-roads town and particularly active, the few Jews still living there spread their sadness, their anxiety and their solitude like a contagious disease. The Temple had now been destroyed some eighteen months, and every Jewish face bore the marks of continued suffering and recent mourning, which had not yet penetrated the depths of their conscious.

Had it not been for the activities of the Greeks and the Syrians, Flavius Silva might well have imagined that as the head of affairs in Judaea he was really the keeper of a cemetery.

He had a need of action, and watching over the new religious schools set up by the people who escaped from the destruction of the Temple was no answer to it. He found the old Jews harmless enough. There were of course one or two outbreaks, particularly near the Dead Sea, but nothing serious. The Zealots had found a place of refuge among the mountains of the desert, but there were very few of them, and they were cut off from the rest of the nation.

Silva did not understand the order he had just received from Vespasian to capture at all costs the fortress of Masada where the remaining Jewish soldiers had entrenched themselves. He knew that some hundred or so determined fighters had taken up their position there, and that from time to time they came down from their mountain to harry Roman convoys; but in fact this only made part of the desert unsettled.

Perhaps Vespasian wanted only to keep Silva busy, and so had given him an operation to keep his men in shape. No matter, if the emperor wanted to destroy the last nest of Jewish resistance, then he had to be satisfied quickly. The year 72 was coming to an end, so the operation had to be finished before the summer of 73.

The Roman general staff was quickly summoned, but they were less optimistic than Silva. Masada could be taken only by surprise, and this was no longer likely. A drawn-out siege was proposed by several officers. Silva rejected the idea since, in the first place, he had information that Masada had considerable reserves, and secondly the Roman army could not afford to mark time, under a leaden sky, while the people resisting it died of starvation.

Silva decided to lead an army of 10,000 men personally, with an additional 5,000 Jewish slaves whose task it would be to keep the Romans supplied with water and to build the huge installations that would be necessary.

When the Roman general arrived at the base of the fortress he realized that it was going to be a long business. While his camp was being erected, sheltered from the south wind, he gave orders that patrols should be sent off in every direction. Their mission was less to establish contact with the Jews than to discover the precise topography of the citadel and to find out how their defences lay. Silva could not suppress a familiar feeling of pride, one he felt every time the Roman army set in motion its organization and its splendour. His men arrived in cohorts, one after the other. Every man seemed to obey natural laws, to do exactly what his leaders expected of him. The first had already pitched their tents, others had scarcely arrived, others were drawn out in the distance in a long line that gleamed with the flash of their arms. But it seemed to Silva that in spite of the insignia that flapped in the desert wind, and in spite of the calm, impeccable, almost mechanical deployment of the Roman forces, there was unspoken anxiety in the ranks, beginning with the general staff. They were far beneath sea level, and he wondered whether his men also felt hemmed in. He was attacked, too, by agonizing uncertainty as to the chances the army had of beating—in a few weeks—the combined resistance of the Jews and this natural colossus.

All night Silva listened to the long moaning of the cold wind rushing to dissipate the daily heat that still lingered among the mountains of Moab. He thought about the men he had sent to look for the secret of the Jewish defence, and began to have fears about the contents of the report they would bring him tomorrow. No sooner had he fallen asleep than his aide came to wake him.

All the patrols had now returned and the winter sun was already high in the sky. The commanders gathered around the Roman general and gave their reports.

The first soldier to speak calmly detailed what he had been able to learn about the eastern face of Masada. Attack in this direction would be impossible. Access to the fortress was covered by a narrow path which rose up among the rocks like a snake. It was impossible for two men to advance side by side. Moreover, for two thirds of the way the path was within reach of the defensive wall of the citadel. Huge stones were lined up on the edge of the precipice and a child could send them down on the attackers. Finally, it would be impossible to bring up any sort of war engine. Only infantry could be used.

The Roman dropped back into the ranks while the man responsible for the exploration of the north came forward. What he said was discouraging. There was a dizzy drop, and not even a goat could get up to the Jewish position. Moreover the defenders had three lines of defence. There was no possibility of attack on that face.

The centurion who had attempted to approach from the south said in a clear, unhesitating voice, that attack was also impossible from that side. There was a bastion hollowed out of the very rock which commanded a smooth and long slope. No machine could approach that bastion.

Silva then turned towards the officer in command of the patrols who had gone to explore the western side of the Masada. He came forward and hesitated a little before speaking. He thought for a few seconds and then said that the western side of the fortress seemed to be as inaccessible as the others. The ground was dusty, the rocks numerous and the difference in height at least two hundred cubits (some three hundred and thirty feet). But he added that they had noticed a sort of promontory which overhung the least elevated part of Masada. Even so, the valley between the two points was very deep. He hesitated for a moment and then said that the promontory was of white stone.

Next day Silva set out at dawn in that direction. He met the first convoys of Jewish slaves as they were arriving. He felt that this manpower would be useful. After two hours he reached the top of the white promontory. He saw the huge stronghold he had to take, noticing also that the Zealots did not seem to be short of water, food or weapons. Children went to and fro, fires were burning, and at each corner sentries watched over the outer wall with its casemates. But Silva was particularly interested in the valley. He stayed for a long time and looked at the deep drop.

A few days later, when all the auxiliary troops had arrived, he ordered his best troops to attack on the west face. The result did not surprise Silva. Only one in five soldiers survived the mad attempt.

Then the Roman general unveiled his plan to his general staff. First of all the ten thousand men had to be divided into eight camps around the fortress. Silva would have his own quarters at the foot of the north face. Then a wall would be built all round Masada so that the Jews would not be able to escape. There would be twelve towers on the wall and it would be between two and three cubits (forty to sixty inches) thick. According to Silva's calculations, the wall would be about twenty stades long—in other words, almost two miles. Then the Roman army would build a ramp for access.

Before they left to give the first orders, Silva's officers looked at each other without understanding what their superior had in mind when he talked about building a ramp. The ground did not lend itself to this manoeuvre, which was a classic of the Roman army. Regardless, thousands of slaves would be forced to form a huge chain for bringing water, cement, stone and wood to the site for underpinning the enormous siege wall.

*   *   *

Eleazar ben Ya'ir loved to linger on the upper terrace of Herod's villa in the northern part of the citadel of Masada—primarily because he was able to see what was going on in Silva's camp and watch the progress being made on the wall with which the Roman general thought he would surround Masada. Eleazar was full of pity for the Jews who had to act as beasts of burden for the Romans, but he was proud that he and his friends had chosen war to the end rather than slavery. Eleazar also liked this palace because it was sheltered from the south wind which swept the region all day. Herod's architects had designed the royal residence well. From here one could see the whole of the Dead Sea, and in the far distance the mountains of Moab.

The Roman camp, with Silva and his officers, was within calling distance of the besieged. Every day when the Roman guard was relieved, insults were bandied from both sides. Calls to surrender and promises of slaughter followed one another. But after a few hours the fighters got tired, and until the next guard took over, the only thing that broke the silence was the noise of daily life in the two camps.

Before he went to give his orders for the following days, Eleazar ran his eyes slowly round the whole of the encircling wall. He shrugged his shoulders as he left his vantage point. He thought that the siege was useless. The Zealots would never give up, their reserves were inexhaustible and any frontal attack was doomed to failure. On the other hand, in a few weeks summer would soon be there, and the immense Roman army would literally suffocate under its tents. The sun would ravage Silva as it had done general Gallus who, seven years ago, had abandoned the siege of Jerusalem without a fight. Silva would go away crestfallen and tell his emperor that Masada could not be taken. Eleazar could then undertake the reconquest of Judaea, re-establish Jewish independence and, above all, rebuild the Temple of God, well-protected in the midst of His People.

Roman patrols regularly tested the Jewish defences and the Zealots made sallies from time to time, but nothing of any note took place for several weeks.

On one particular day, Eleazar was urgently summoned to the south bastion. The officer of the guard had noticed some unusual activity on the white promontory. The leader of Masada saw that thousands of slaves were going up in a long brown line to the top which, at that point, dominated the Jewish citadel. Eleazar remained silent for a long time. He was trying to understand the manoeuvre. He could see that the prisoners were heavily laden with a variety of materials, but he could not imagine what sort of fortification the Romans would be able to build at that point. Any new arrangement on the promontory would be a pointless duplication of the surrounding wall. Moreover, if Silva imagined that he was going to be able to take advantage of the superior height of the promontory, so as to bombard Masada, he was making a grave mistake, since no engine was powerful enough to send even very light missiles the distance that at this point separated the surrounding wall from Masada.

Towards the middle of the day the Zealots were amazed to see that the five thousand chained Jews, beaten by armed Romans, were carrying out what amounted to sapper work along the white promontory. In a few hours tons of earth had been hurled into the valley under a cloud of yellow dust. Below, other workers began to press down the soil, adding water brought by a huge chain of men from the north camp. Eleazar realized that Silva was trying to build an assault ramp. It was madness, for as soon as the Romans came within the reach of the Jewish archers they would be cut to pieces.

The work went on for three weeks. The people in Masada spent their free time watching the progress of this huge enterprise without experiencing the least anxiety. The long confrontation with the Romans had calmed the fears they had felt on the first few days when the imperial forces had been deployed. Now the Romans were a part of the landscape and their work—like that of ants—was as useless as their tents would soon be in the summer sun.

Gradually the promontory was being nibbled away by the workers. The assault ramp was taking shape. Eleazar estimated that it was four hundred cubits (some six hundred and sixty feet) wide.

One day the officer in command of the south bastion thought that the enemy was within arrow shot. Without waiting he gave the order for the first salvo. It was victory. Some men died with their arms spread out as on a cross or twisted up in agony under their wounds. But when the first feeling of satisfaction had passed, the officer realized that only Jewish slaves had been harmed. The Romans hastily made themselves shelters which both allowed them to survey the work and protect themselves. Eleazar ordered a stop to the arrows.

At the beginning of spring, when the first yellow flowers began to show on the top of Masada, The Romans had almost finished their preparations. The ramp was as broad as it was long and rested against the west side of Masada. Everyone could see the difference in height between the ramp and the casemate wall was some eight cubits (one hundred and thirty-three feet). The Romans could never bring up a machine that tall.

But a few days later there appeared, pushed by a crowd of men covered in dust, under the rhythmic orders of the centurions, a huge tower on wheels. The Jewish defenders looked at each other in amazement and began to bend their bows. But when the tower had been pushed a few yards the ramp collapsed and the Roman work fell into the ravine, as a cry of joy issued from Masada.

During the following day or two the Romans tried to reinforce their ramp. They installed a cemented apron which gave it the appearance of a huge windowless house. Scarcely had a new Roman tower made its appearance than a hail of arrows shot down many Roman soldiers and Jewish slaves. But the tower continued to advance and was now vertical with the ramparts of the fortress. As the Roman archers gave protection, the sappers brought into action an enormous battering-ram against the outer wall.

This went on for two days. The Roman losses were enormous but Silva was imperturbable and ordered that the operation be continued. The Jewish resistance was all the more intense since the attack was restricted to one spot only. Eleazar ordered that a second wall be built to duplicate the rampart under attack. When the Romans, yelling in triumph, saw the protecting wall disintegrating, the Jews mocked them and retreated behind their second line of defence. Silva immediately ordered a new attack, but Eleazar was rich in the experience he had acquired, and had had the second wall built with clay that was still damp, so that each blow of the Roman machine reinforced the work rather than weakened it.

Then Silva ordered his archers to try and set fire to the beams supporting the wall by raining down a flight of burning arrows. At first everyone thought that the operation was going to be successful. But Silva, who was at the foot of the tower protected by his bodyguard, was enraged when he saw that the wind was not favourable to the Romans. The ceaseless south wind was blowing with fury. The Roman tower itself began to blaze, and the Jews began to intone thanksgivings. Silva called for reinforcements and left the surrounding wall unprotected on the other fronts. It mattered little if a few Zealots fled.

In the Jewish camp they continued to offer prayers of thanksgiving to God. They were sure that it was at His wish that the wind had blown twice as hard just when the pagans began their manoeuvre. They embraced each other, jumped for joy and showed each other the fire arrows caught on the Roman machine.

Suddenly a disturbing silence fell over the battlefield. The Roman flags were still, then hung sadly at the masts. The beds of jonquils—the pride of the besieged—danced no more. The flames hesitantly picked up. The sun disappeared behind the white promontory. The desert no longer blew the wind of Roman defeat.

At first the noise was imperceptible, then a little rustling, and at last a heavy caress. The wind had changed. It was coming from the north. The mountains of Moab were today warmer than the desert of Judaea. As night fell the last wall of the last square of the defenders of the new Temple finished burning. The Jews were lost.

Silva wisely stopped operations and gave orders for the attack which he preferred to launch the following day. The defenders of Masada and their families gathered round a large fire. No one had really given up hope, but they were all afraid of tomorrow. They were hoping for a new display, a new victorious initiative from their leader. But Eleazar no longer believed in victory. He only had one thought from the very moment that resistance became impossible. He did not want his men one day to be like the unfortunate men they saw for weeks on end acting as beasts of burden for the Romans. Eleazar knew that there was only one way to make an end of it: collective suicide. Could he persuade his men that liberty and death were better than servitude?

*   *   *

Samuel ben Ezra sat close to his leader. He was surrounded by his wife and children, and Simeon ben Yeozer the priest. They expected words of comfort. Eleazar spoke:

'My loyal followers, long ago we resolved to serve neither the Romans nor anyone else but only God, who alone is the true and righteous Lord of men: now the time has come that bids us prove our determination by our deeds. At such a time we must not disgrace ourselves; hitherto we have never submitted to slavery, even when it brought no danger with it: we must not choose slavery now, and with it penalties that will mean the end of everything if we fall alive into the hands of the Romans. For we were the first of all to revolt, and shall be the last to break off the struggle. And I think it is God who has given us this privilege, that we can die nobly and as free men, unlike others who were unexpectedly defeated. In our case it is evident that daybreak will end our resistance, but we are free to choose an honourable death with our loved ones. This our enemies cannot prevent, however earnestly they may pray to take us alive; nor can we defeat them in battle...

'Let our wives die unabused, our children without knowledge of slavery: after that, let us do each other an ungrudging kindness, preserving our freedom as a glorious winding-sheet. But first let our possessions and the whole fortress go up in flame: it will be a bitter blow to the Romans, that I know, to find our persons beyond their reach and nothing left for them to loot. One thing only let us spare—our store of food: it will bear witness when we are dead to the fact that we perished, not through want but because, as we resolved at the beginning, we chose death rather than slavery.' (*The Jewish War.*)

No one had counted on words of death. Samuel looked at his children and could not imagine obeying such inhuman orders. But although many were weeping, no one dared contradict Eleazar. He was astonished at the fear his words had caused, and took up his speech in a different tone. It was less friendly and more authoritarian. He knew that he was right.

Eleazar could have talked for hours, but he was interrupted by his Zealot friends who were embracing each other, in tears, as they decided to give up their lives. Bachelor soldiers began to set fire to the citadel and each family drew aside to carry out the deadly deed. The last embraces were the longest, but already cries pierced the night. Heads of family killed the members of their family. Ten men appointed for the task went among the groups and killed the less brave. They finally met after many hours, alone with their leader in the midst of the flames. They drew lots for the one who was to survive and kill himself. It all happened very quickly. In a matter of seconds the one chosen by fate found himself with his bloody sword in his hand, alone in a sea of flame. He quickly went round the dwelling places. Nothing lived, nothing moved. He killed himself without hesitation.

Daylight began to spread over Masada. The Romans threw themselves in force into the breach, swords at the ready, bows bent for action. They looked in all directions, afraid of a ruse. They were surrounded by flames, and a curtain of smoke hid the spectacle of desolation awaiting them.

A centurion who was impatient and wanted to come to blows jumped through the fire into the centre of the citadel. He let out a savage cry calling the enemy to fight. Nothing moved. Two women in rags then came out of a hiding place and told the Romans what had happened during the night.

Gradually, struggling against the flames, the Romans found most of the dead Zealots. There was no shout of triumph to mark the victory. All the Romans, and Silva in particular, were overcome by admiration and respect.

*   *   *

Hundreds of Zealots now wandered, devoid of any aim, through captive Judaea. They did not know where to go or where to take their will to resist. The Jewish state was plunged into nothingness. Galilee, which was usually so carefree and happy, barely breathed any more. The coastal towns were dead, in spite of the artificial activity brought to them by the merchants and the Romans. The mountains of Judaea were crossed only by Roman patrols, and Jerusalem was devoid of any life.

The few remaining leaders of the party founded by Judas the Galilean some eighty years earlier ordered that open resistance be abandoned within the boundaries of the Promised Land. The idea of the Diaspora taking up the fight slowly gained currency. There were new, lively forces there. Rich, powerful Jews might in their turn revolt and take over the torch of the conquered Jewish fighters.

But Rome was still there and growing in power. Vespasian had died in 79 and been succeeded by his son Titus. The conqueror of Jerusalem was an exemplary emperor. He was called 'the delight of the human race.' But his reign was short. In 81 his brother Domitian took over, and for the next fifteen years he was a cruel and ambitious ruler. When he died, the Flavian dynasty, which had devoted so much energy to the destruction of Jewish sovereignty, perished with him. The end of the Flavians facilitated a considerable increase in the dynamism of the Diaspora and accelerated the movement of emigration among the Jews.

The land of Israel had possibly been depopulated for revolutionary strategic reasons, but certainly also for economic motives. Famine was the fate of all. But in the Diaspora a much more satisfactory state of affairs existed, and Judaism was adopted by a considerable number of converts. Alexandria continued to contain a rich Jewish community intellectually superior to that of the Holy Land. In Mesopotamia (modern Iraq), new emigrants went to join those who, almost a thousand years previously, had refused to leave Babylon and return to the Promised Land. The Zealots followed the migrations. They went to North Africa, Greece and Cyprus.

The masters of the religious schools did not conceal their concern. The depopulation of the Holy Land spelled the end of the material possession of the country by the Jews. Rabbi Johanan and his followers had shown the dangerous nature of warlike nationalism, but the heads of all the schools believed in the importance of the physical presence of the Jews in their land, even in a less impressive role.

When Trajan became emperor in 98, Judaism represented the most important movement concerned with thought in the whole of the Roman world.

The Zealots tried to waken the Jewish communities of a happy and contented Empire to the idea of rebellion. Almost thirty years after the event, ex-soldiers crossed the Euphrates and went into the Parthian Empire to take their revolutionary message to the Jews. In handing over to his disciple Gamaliel, Johanan ben Zakkai inaugurated a tradition which is at the base of a lasting intellectualization of Jewish life: every master of Judaism, from the day that Johanan began to teach, has passed on the essential elements of his knowledge to his best disciples. And they, in their turn, have passed on their knowledge to their successors, and so it will be to the end of time. But without exception the students of the Law expounded new ideas which they discovered 'unpolished' in the teaching of their masters, and which they were able to confirm by reference to the Torah itself.

Beginning with the year 70, the class of teachers replaced that of the priests, for since the destruction of the Temple they had no further function. The Jews might well retain the memory of the priestly class, but they still had no current *raison d'être*.

Nothing had destined Akiba, son of Joseph, for rabbinical investiture. He was a poor young man of modest origins, and was only twenty years old when the Temple was burned. He seemed to have no ambition other than to marry the sister of a friend who was a wise and rich man. This young woman would only consent to marry him if he went and studied the Law. Akiba agreed, secretly married the woman he loved, and went off to study. He came back twelve years later followed by twelve thousand pupils, saw his wife once more, then went off for a further twelve years after which he came back followed by twenty-four thousand pupils.

Rabbi Akiba's teaching was classical. In particular he took up and developed the teaching of Hillel when he said, 'Love your neighbour as yourself, that is the great principle of the Law.' He also said, 'The rampart of wisdom is silence.' But he attributed extraordinary power to the individual. He taught that 'God foresees all, nevertheless man has free will.' Akiba was responsible for a very individual interpretation of the Torah. In his theory the sacred letters in the text of the Law had each a special value, and that when they were put into a different order it was possible—and permissible for a learned person—to discern different levels of understanding of the Divine word. Thus the roots of the Cabbala were planted by Akiba. Even so, his teaching was marked by infinite confidence in God and His plan for Israel. One day, when he was travelling with other scholars of Judaism, they heard shouts in the distance and light-hearted songs coming from a town of idolatrous people. Akiba's companions burst out into sobs, lamenting such an abomination. Akiba, however, laughed at them.

'Why are you weeping?' he asked his friends.

'What!' the others replied. 'These idolatrous people burn incense and pray to images, they live in security and pleasure while our Temple, —the repository of the true God—is destroyed by flames. Should we not weep?'

'That is precisely why I laugh,' replied Akiba. 'If the people who disobey God's will are so happy in part, think what the happiness must be that is stored up for those who carry out His will.'

Akiba and his friends were soon followed by a vast multitude of pupils. The new century was ten years old, and in a few years the Torah had become the sole and constant occupation of the Jews living in Judaea, who influenced in their wake all the Diaspora. Of course the memory of the splendour of the Sanctuary of Israel, destroyed almost forty years earlier, was still alive in the Jewish consciousness, but as Rabbi Johanan had wished, obsession with study had replaced hope of an immediate reconstruction of the Temple.

Rabbi Akiba himself made a series of journeys to Rome, Babylon, Galatia and Phrygia in Asia Minor. He met the heads of all the Jewish communities. He taught the principles of Jewish knowledge, but at the same time he took stock of the potential strength of the Jews. Under the pretext of teaching, the Zealot leaders followed in Akiba's steps. The hatred of the Romans which coloured their words at first astonished the Jewish communities, but soon they appreciated the justness of their argument. Judaism did not enjoy the position it deserved in the civilized world. The Holy Land was occupied and pagans ruled uncontested and imposed their laws. But the great revolutionary motive remained the same. The walls of the destroyed Temple had to be rebuilt. Following Akiba's example, the most fervent worshippers of God began to hope again. One sabbath evening a rabbi saw one of his masters unintentionally tilt a lighted lamp, which was forbidden. He wrote rather naively: 'Ishmael, son of Elisha, has tilted the light on the Sabbath. When the Temple is rebuilt, he will have to offer an expiatory sacrifice.' (*Talmud*, *Shabbat* 12b.) The time for the rebuilding was therefore near.

During this time Trajan ruled successfully. He promulgated social measures which protected widows and orphans, and he had food distributed to the poor. But in common with all Roman emperors, he dreamed of following in the footsteps of Alexander and of taking Roman civilization to the heart of India. Barring the route to the Far East were the Parthians, those invincible warriors who regularly stopped the Roman legions.

In 115 the Romans once again had to confront the Parthians, and the war dragged on for several years. The Zealots chose that moment to launch the most serious general revolt since the rule of the emperors began.

In Cyrenia (now Libya) the enraged Jews attacked the garrisons and pagan communities. Thousands of dead littered the path of the Zealots towards Jerusalem. A man called Andreas was at the head of the movement. Revolt broke out simultaneously in Egypt, and the Jews practically overran the country (apart from Alexandria, which had, in fact, a large Jewish population on which the routed Roman legions took their vengeance). The Jews in Cyprus destroyed everything in their path, led by a man called Artemion.

East of the Euphrates the Jewish communities of Mesopotamia supported the Parthians and fought with unequalled frenzy. Trajan realized that there was a master plan behind the revolution and that if the Jews, who were practically in control of Cyrenia and Egypt, joined up with those of the Euphrates, Rome's power could well be seriously threatened. All the southern Mediterranean would belong to a new Jewish

Empire. Instead of reaching India, the Romans would have to fall back on Europe and give up once and for all their great Asian and African design. The union of these two revolutionary movements could only be made at Jerusalem. From an ideological and strategic point of view the new Jewish initiative could only have as its goal the ancient city of David. The troops would have to hold the former province of Judaea and terrorize the Jews who still lived there to prevent revolt. Trajan realized that the war with the Parthians must be stopped immediately. He entered into negotiations and arranged for the emblems which the Romans had taken in the course of recent fighting to be handed back to the enemy. He also had to appoint a general to Judaea who would be tough. Trajan thought first of Hadrian, who was in command in Syria, but he was not easily controllable—not a man to be a tool in the emperor's hands, ready to do his bidding. The emperor therefore appointed a man from Mauretania—present-day Tunisia and Algeria—who had been condemned for treason and had since been in disgrace. Lusius Quietus was well known for his cruelty. There was a régime of bloody terror in Judaea. Even the smallest assemblies were forbidden, and the hand of repression fell on anyone who dared keep in touch with the progress of the Jewish revolt.

All the same, at Bne Brak, a small town near the Mediterranean coast where Akiba had built his school, the news of the violent awakening of the Jews was received with joy. Many of the men who sat at Akiba's feet were old soldiers, veterans of the defence of Jerusalem, and now their joy was a little tempered by the thought that this revolution had come too late. If only the Diaspora had come to the aid of beleaguered Jerusalem, if only Simon ben Giora's hopes had been realized, the Temple would still be standing.

During the course of the year 117, it became obvious that although the Empire was swept by fire and bloodshed, Judaea was calm. There was not the slightest hint of revolt, and Quietus' fanatic authority covered the whole of the province. When Judaea was fighting in 70 the Diaspora did not move. Now the exact opposite was true. Because of the lack of initiative of the Jews of the Holy Land, the revolt of the Diaspora was going to fail. The fighters in the West would never be able to join up with those in the East.

Hadrian, who was still at his post in Syria, noted with anxiety the development of Quietus' policy of terror and his ambitions He thought that such a man was capable of preventing him from becoming emperor. The Jewish revolt was at this moment almost under control. Pitiless repression was the order of the day throughout the Empire. The victory honours would go to Quietus.

But when Trajan died, Hadrian was proclaimed emperor by his troops. Immediately he focused his attention on Caesarea, where Quietus was finishing off his work of preventive repression.

In the face of this terrible situation, the rabbis of the religious schools used the only weapons they had. As a sign of mourning they forbade fiancés to wear the traditional crown. They also forbade the teaching of Greek to Jewish children, since it was a symbol of the will to compromise Jewish intelligence.

One day two Jewish resistance workers, Julian and Pappus, who were brothers, were brought before Quietus. He said to them:

'If you are of the Chosen People, let your God come and save you from my hands as He once saved the three Jews who fell into the hands of Nebuchadnezzar.'

'Those three men,' replied Julian and Pappus, 'were truly righteous, and Nebuchadnezzar a perfect king who deserved a miracle. But you are a tryrant unworthy of a miracle. If we deserve death in the sight of Heaven and you do not kill us, God has quite sufficient means at His disposal; bears, lions, serpents, and scorpions in great numbers to kill us. If you kill us, God will one day demand an account from you of our blood that you will have shed.' (*Ecclesiastes Rabbah.*) Quietus did not have the time to put the two men to death. At the end of this exchange, assassins hired by Hadrian threw themselves on him and killed him.

*   *   *

Now that he had eliminated Quietus, Hadrian wanted to appear magnanimous. His spirit of adventure, his childish curiosity and his taste for restorations induced him to promise the Jews the rebuilding of the Temple. In this way he wanted to reward the inhabitants of Palestine for having kept quiet during the war that Trajan had been forced to fight throughout the Empire against the Diaspora. Hadrian also remembered with a certain amount of nostalgia the passionate conversations he had had with Rabbi Joshua ben Hanania, the most respected of the Jewish wise men. This venerable man had persuaded Hadrian that God had not turned away from the people of the Jews. Hadrian, in the euphoria which followed his accession, allowed it to be said everywhere that he authorized the criminal and fortuitous act of the Roman soldier who set fire to the

Temple in Jerusalem to be compensated, and that the Jews might rebuild the house of their God.

Jewish hopes were great. It was recalled that the first exile in Babylon lasted for fifty-two years. It was now forty-eight years since Titus had turned Jerusalem into a desert. A few more months and the splendour of Israel would have been recovered. The execution of Quietus was the first pledge of goodwill given to the Jews by Hadrian. Some even said that the very people who destroyed the Temple would rebuild it.

The brothers Julian and Pappus set up collecting centres along the whole of the coast where the Jews, as they returned from exile, might change their money for the gold and silver that would be needed for the Temple worship. But the Jews had many enemies. Chief among these were the Samaritans, who always had reproached the priestly class for refusing to recognize the Temple they had built in their province. The re-establishment of the Jewish sanctuary would mean the opening up of the quarrel once more and the strengthening of their enemies. The Samaritans went to Hadrian and told him:

'If Jerusalem is rebuilt, as the emperor well knows, the Jews will no longer pay either taxes, tribute money or tithes.' (*Midrash Bereshit Rabbah*, LXIV, 10).

The emperor asked what he could do, since the decree had already been announced. The Samaritans replied that all he had to do was to tell them to alter the site or make the building five cubits (a hundred inches) more or less than the original, and they would desist of their own accord.

When the Jews learned about the plot devised by their Samaritan enemies they wept and talked about revolt against the emperor. They turned to Joshua ben Hanania for advice.

'A lion devoured his prey and then found that a bone was stuck in his gullet. He immediately promised a reward to the person who got it out for him. A Swan with a long beak appeared, and removed the bone with its beak. The swan asked for payment. The lion told it to go and boast that it had put its beak in a lion's mouth and had brought it out safe and sound. It is quite enough that we have been involved with this nation and have escaped without harm.' (*Midrash, Bereshit Rabbah*, LXIV, 10).

Even so, Joshua tried to convince Hadrian that he was wrong. He went to see him at Alexandria, but was unable to obtain satisfaction, and Hadrian appointed a budding tyrant, Ticinius Rufus, to Syria. Moreover, Hadrian confirmed the outlawing of circumcision, assemblies for study, and even ritual baths for Jewish women. Finally, since the Jews wanted a Temple at Jerusalem, the emperor announced that he would build one—as he had promised—but the sanctuary would not be consecrated to God but to Capitoline Jupiter, and the city itself would no longer be called Jerusalem but Aelia Capitolina. An equestrian statue of the emperor would adorn the new building.

It was the 9th day of Ab, and Rabbi Akiba and other successors of Johanan stood on the ruins of the Temple. They had torn their clothing and began to lament, when they saw a fox run out of the ruins of the Holy of Holies. They all began to cry except Akiba, who laughed. He asked them why they were weeping, and they answered:

'Should we not weep on the place of which it is said the profane who approaches it will be struck dead? We have seen with our own eyes the fulfilment of these words: Mount Zion in ruins will be over-run by foxes.'

Akiba replied: 'That is exactly why I am laughing. Uriah the priest said: "Zion will be tilled as a field. Jerusalem will become a mound of ruins, and the Temple Mount a wooded height." And Zechariah, son of Berechiah, said: "There shall yet old men and old women dwell in the streets of Jerusalem, and every man with his staff in his hand for very age. And the streets of the city shall be full of boys and girls playing in the streets thereof." As long as Uriah's prophecy remained unfulfilled I was afraid that of Zechariah would not be fulfilled. But now that Uriah's is fulfilled, I know for a certainty that Zechariah's will also be fulfilled literally.'

'Akiba, Akiba,' the others cried, 'you have comforted us, you have comforted us.' (*Talmud*, Maccot 24 a, b.)

Akiba freely expressed the idea that Johanan seemed to have wanted to keep from the people—that the Temple would be rebuilt. The fact that he was so confident was proof that study did not turn a person away from priestly worship, that wise men were priests and that the prayers of the Jews were nationalist slogans. Moreover, it was at this time that the Jews began to add to their daily prayers this invocation which is still recited today: 'Blessed art Thou, O Lord, who in Thy compassion rebuildest Jerusalem.' Thus the misery Titus caused, and the irreparable loss that the disappearance of the Temple represented, always remained in their consciousness.

Hadrian was unable to put his plan into immediate operation. In the spring of 132 a large Jewish army raised by Simon ben Koziba attacked the Roman garrisons and won its first victories. The leader came from Modin, like the Maccabees. He had incredible physical strength and he trained his soldiers as no other Jewish soldiers had ever been trained. The Roman legions were not ready for the attack and were soundly beaten. Simon soon found himself among the ruins of Jerusalem. He had crossed Egypt like lightning and quickly occupied the whole of the province of Judaea.

The suddenness of the attack forced Hadrian to send his best general, Julius Severus, to Palestine: Severus had just defeated the British. But the Jews were better organized that the Romans—due both to Simon's military ability and to the long politico-spiritual preparation that Rabbi Akiba had given to the Jews during his many journeys throughout the Diaspora. But Akiba took the decisive step when the leader of the Jewish revolt came to him at Bne Brak. He described him as the saviour of Israel and called him no longer ben Koziba, but Bar Kochba, son of the star.

Bar Kochba and those who followed him did not aim at the immediate re-establishment of the Temple. Before anything else they intended to make Emperor Hadrian pay dearly for the measures he had taken to finish off the Jews. As long as it was possible to hope for the rebuilding of the Sanctuary of Israel, the motives for revolt were left in a state of suspension. But in 132, the Jews no longer had anything to expect from Rome. Circumcision was outlawed; Jerusalem was to be transformed into a pagan sanctuary surrounded by ruins; Judaea lost its name, and finally the study of the Law was forbidden.

Bar Kochba was a war leader. His first aim was to free Judaea and Jerusalem. Other people might well decide to rebuild the Temple. But in order to get the people to make war, and take up arms against Rome (the oldest remembered all too vividly the massacres that followed the catastrophe of 70), Bar Kochba had to be recognized by all the Jews as the uncontested leader of the nation, a prophet of freedom, and finally accepted as the Messiah of Israel.

But he could not ignore the fact that the disciples of Rabbi Johanan had tried to turn the people away from hoping too impatiently for the advent of the Messiah, and that they had tried to drain this hope of political content by turning it into a quest for spiritual salvation, purposefully avoiding the concrete nature of the liberation from Roman oppression.

In these conditions the new leader of Israel knew that if a popular movement designated him as Messiah, he would risk condemnation by the rabbis. Bar Kochba did not want Israel, at any price, to begin again an experience as bitter as that of the battle of Jerusalem, during which the Jewish defenders had been divided to the point where they waged fratricidal fights instead of keeping their blows for the Romans.

Rabbinical backing was indispensable. It must extend not only to the legitimacy of armed combat, but also to the Messianic nature of the person leading the struggle—otherwise it would be impossible to arouse the people.

More than anyone else, Rabbi Akiba was aware of the drama in preparation. He alone had to decide. His choice was critical. If he decided to have nothing to do with Bar Kochba, then he abandoned the people of Israel and weakened even further the chances of the success of an attempted revolt. If, on the other hand, he decided to support the man whose name meant son of the star, he would have to recognize him as God's messenger, the saving Messiah. In that case, Akiba would give a new meaning to the teaching of his predecessors and would lead the whole of Israel into an adventure which, if it failed, would signify the end of the People of God.

Ironically Rabbi Johanan's admonition that Judaism could be kept out of harm's way if Jews turned their energies to study, helped resolve Rabbi Akiba's dilemma. Akiba knew that the Romans had just forbidden meetings for study. Whether Bar Kochba's revolt developed or whether, through lack of rabbinical support, it was a dismal failure, the result would probably be the same: the end of Israel. It was of little importance whether Israel perished because she was prevented from studying the Law or because the revolt was crushed in bloodshed. And after all, if the Jews were united they would perhaps this time have a chance of winning.

The news that Akiba had recognized Bar Kochba as the Messiah spread throughout the Empire. In Palestine and east of the Euphrates, whole Jewish communities were bristling with emotion.

All Akiba's disciples were gathered around him. They only needed a word from him to jump into the revolutionary camp and ignore the teachings about prudence which, since the time of Johanan ben Zakkai, had been their daily bread. They all felt very keenly the inhuman restraint that had been imposed on them by their masters for several decades. Now, thanks to Akiba, two traditional streams in Israel were once more to combine: love of God and freedom of man.

There was complete silence when Bar Kochba entered the large hall of the school at Bne Brak. He was covered in dust and his sword was in his hand, but his eyes shone, and he smiled. Akiba rose slowly, and said, 'See, a star has risen out of Jacob.' Then after a moment's hesitation he added, 'Here is the king, the Messiah.' The enthusiasm was extraordinary. The students of Bne Brak rushed weeping to these warriors, embraced them and asked for arms. No one heard Rabbi Johanan ben Torta go up to his master, Rabbi Akiba, and say to him: 'Akiba, the grass will have grown between your jaws before the Messiah comes.' (*Midrash*, II, 2, 4.) Without further delay he bent over his book once more, ignoring the warlike agitation taking place in this house of study and peace. Akiba would fight with the means at his disposal. He decided to disregard the Roman ban and assemble his numerous disciples for the study and development of God's Torah. When Julius Severus learned that the wise men of Bne Brak had recognized the leader of the rebels as their king, he decided to wipe them out. Between the Passover and the Feast of Tabernacles he executed all the students he could still find and imprisoned Akiba. For many months the highest Jewish spiritual authority languished in a Roman prison. Severus hoped that Akiba would be shown to the Roman crowd in the course of Hadrian's certain triumph, as Simon ben Giora had been, before being put to death publicly.

Bar Kochba was now master of Jerusalem, where Hadrian had had no time to build his pagan temple. He was in the middle of the ruins that covered the remains of those exemplary fighters who had fought to the limits of human endurance. But the new leader of the rediscovered Jewish nation ordered retreat. The city of David could not be defended. The soldiers who were able to uproot a Lebanon cedar from a galloping horse evacuated the city, for which they had all sworn to die, without a fight. Bar Kochba decided to give battle to the Romans on the mountains of Judaea, the 'royal mountain' that cut the province in two from north to south and consequently reduced the possibility of frontal attack. The leader of the revolt set up his headquarters on top of an observatory where he could see equally well what was taking place on both sides of the ridge. This stronghold was called Bethar. From here one could also see Jerusalem, which was very important for the morale of the men. The citadel was protected by fifty support points scattered among the valleys and on the hills commanding the approach to Bethar. In the many villages throughout the territory controlled by the Jews everything was geared to resistance, though under the influence of Akiba's disciples schools were opened everywhere: so the Jews continued their study of the Law, without which the armed combat they were engaged in would have no meaning. Their revolt would have had no sense if Bar Kochba had not been the Messiah. The proof of the rightness of their cause and of the Messiahship of Bar Kochba was demonstrated by the presence among their ranks of men such as Rabbi Eleazar ben Modin, Bar Kochba's uncle. He spent the whole day in prayer. In a hair shirt, and covered with ashes, he spoke to the God of Israel. 'Master of the worlds, do not give justice today.' Evidently no one asked why Rabbi Eleazar wanted God to put off the day of justice. They all thought that it was the day of death that Rabbi Eleazar wanted to put off. No one imagined that the defeat of Bar Kochba might mark the day of justice.

The Jews' religious fervour was intense. Feasts, sabbaths and the slightest requirement of the Torah were observed. As he went to prayer one morning Rabbi Eleazar looked reprovingly at two Jewish soldiers who were polishing a Roman vase that had been carried off in a raid. The vase was carved with a pigeon on it—and the Law forbade the reproduction of any living thing.

Julius Severus saw that the Jews occupied the backbone of the province of Judaea. Supplies came from Ein Gedi on the Dead Sea, so his officers advised him to attack from the south in order to strangle the Jews by cutting them off from the oasis that guaranteed their supplies of water and food. But Severus was inspired by the example of Flavius Silva who had taken Masada, and thought it undignified that a Roman army should not win by force of arms. He therefore decided to attack Bethar directly.

But the battle went badly for the Romans, who fell victim to a number of victorious sallies by Bar Kochba's men. The Jews resisted for nearly three-and-a-half years and Severus contemplated giving up the siege. But just as he was preparing to order the retreat, an old Samaritan came up to him and asked permission to try one last ruse to bring down Bethar.

With the agreement of the Roman general, the old man crossed the lines and entered the citadel. He went up to Rabbi Eleazar, who was at prayer. 'He pretended to whisper something in his ear, and immediately the inhabitants of the town got hold of him and brought him before Bar Kochba. "We saw this old man," they said, "talking with your uncle."

"What did you talk to him about, and what did he say to you?" asked Bar Kochba.

' "If I tell you," replied the Samaritan, "the emperor will kill me.

If I do not tell you, you will kill me. I would rather die at the emperor's hand than yours. Well, your uncle confided to me that he would hand over the town." Bar Kochba immediately went to Rabbi Eleazar ben Modin and asked what the Samaritan had talked to him about.

' "Nothing," replied Eleazar.

' "And what did you say to him?"

' "Again, nothing." Bar Kochba gave Eleazar a kick that killed him. At once a voice was heard:

' "Woe to the unfaithful shepherds who abandon their sheep. Woe to his arm and to his right eye. May his arm wither and his right eye be obscured." ' (*Talmud*, Gittin 57a.)

The news caused consternation in he Jewish camp. Bar Kochba had killed his holy uncle and God had shown His presence in announcing the fall of the fortress. The bravest Jews were in despair, but remained at their posts. Others began to flee or take refuge in the caves of Nahal Hever.

The attack the Romans now launched was to be the last. The citadel that God no longer inhabited fell into the hands of the legions, and Bar Kochba himself was captured and beheaded. His head was taken to Hadrian.

'Who killed him?' asked the emperor.

'I did,' said a Samaritan.

'Show me the back of the head,' said Hadrian. They showed it to him and found that there was a snake coiled up on it. 'If God had not killed him,' said the emperor, 'no one would have put an end to it.' (*Midrash*, on Echa II 2).

The repression that followed was terrible. A wave of blood washed through the valleys of Judaea. Jews fled from all parts. The Promised Land was soon empty of any Jews' presence. The few Jewish intellectuals who had remained aloof from the fighting all left the place of martyrdom, and the others were put to death, Rabbi Akiba first of all.

Akiba never knew the outcome of Bar Kochba's Messianic adventure. He died for the study of the Law, not for attempting to force the fate of Israel by taking arms to rebuild the Temple.

After the failure of Bar Kochba, Akiba's example led many of his followers to die also for the study of the Law, the unique dimension of the Jewish being, when Israel lived without a Temple.

Rabbi Hanina ben Teradion died in this way. 'The Romans encountered Rabbi Hanina ben Teradion seated, teaching and concerning himself with the Torah in his heart. He was led out, wrapped in the roll of the Torah, surrounded by faggots in which the branches were still green and which were set alight. They brought swabs of wool soaked in water which they put on his heart so that his soul did not depart too quickly. His daughter said to him, "Father, must I see you in this state?" He replied, "If I were burned alone I should be sad, but seeing that I am burned and the book of the Torah is with me, the one who acknowledges the offence done to the Torah will also acknowledge the offence done to me." His pupils said to him, "Master, what do you see?"

' "The parchment burns but the letters fly away."

' "Then you also, open your mouth, that the fire goes in and your soul flies away."

' "May He who gave it to me take it back. I will not do it myself." Then the executioner said to him: "My master, if I increase the heat and take away the swabs of wool on your heart, will you take me to the world which is coming?"

' "Yes."

' "Swear to me."

And the rabbi swore. Immediately the executioner increased the heat, took the woollen swabs away from his heart and quickly his soul went forth. The executioner jumped into the fire and fell as well. And a Divine voice sounded, saying:

' "Rabbi Hanina and his executioner will have a share in the world which is to come."

'Rabbi Judah the Prince wept and said: "There are some who gain eternity in an hour, and others in how many years!" ' (Talmud, Aboda Zara 18a.)

The Roman army had won a victory, but tens of thousands of men had fallen in the third Jewish war. Neither Severus nor Rufus had a triumph, and when Hadrian went to the Senate to give an account of the victory in Judaea he did not say the traditional words that all victorious generals used since time immemorial when they began their speech to the Roman assembly: 'If you and your children are well, I am glad of it. I and my army are well.'

8 Life in the Diaspora

A lone Jew decided to flee the country that the Romans now called Palestine. There was nothing to keep him there. The Temple had been destroyed, there was no hope of a national revival and no hope of a happy life, simple and anonymous. Famine hit all the Jews. Suspicion destroyed human contacts. Even the religious schools, which still held out hope for some, were open only to an intellectual élite to which this man did not belong. In any case, their activities were still clandestine. The outlawing of anything that might recall organized Jewish life still weighed heavily on the people whose alliance with God seemed broken.

But rabbis disguised as merchants went up and down the country, from door to door, preaching that to abandon the Holy Land was the greatest sin. They taught the following:

'A man will live in Palestine, even in a town where there is a majority of Gentiles, rather than abroad in an entirely Jewish city. To live in Palestine is like carrying out all the commandments of the Torah, and the person who is buried in Palestine is like one buried under the altar.'

The rabbis realized that the massacres which followed the three wars that Judaism had just suffered and the current tendency to leave Palestine would result in a dispersal with no hope of a return to the land where God lived. They meant to encourage marriages between Jews who intended to settle in Palestine. They taught that a man is as important as all the works of creation put together. Moreover they forbade the Jews to sell their land to Gentiles. They reminded them that the land was exceptionally fertile, and declared that the Jews should devote themselves to it and in this way come back to their secular vocation as farmers.

But the lone Jew resisted all the rabbis' injunctions. He wanted to finish with the ungrateful land that he loved so much. The death of Hadrian and the favourable measures taken towards the Jews by Antoninus did nothing to make him change his mind. What did it matter to him if the Jews were once again permitted to carry out their Law and study it,

or even circumcise their sons, when they had to live among the ruins of
the Jewish nation under the yoke of the oppressor?

To avoid meeting Roman patrols, and because he was one of the
few people to escape after the Bar Kochba rebellion, he decided to follow
the Dead Sea on the east and to slip between the mountains of Moab to
the south, towards Egypt. Without once turning back he reached
Jericho, but the gentle air and freshness of the palm groves aroused no
feelings of peace or security in him. He spent the night there without
speaking to a soul, and the next day he continued his journey to the East.
He passed Qumran where the Essenes had been established before they
joined with the Zealots in the great war against Rome, but it had no effect
on him. In the deep south he crossed the Jordan where it joins the Dead
Sea. On his right now were the mountains of Moab. Before going south,
as if he were being driven by some age old primitive force, he climbed
one mountain, then two, and a few hours later was on the summit of
Mount Nebo. He knew that from this spot Moses saw the land that God
had promised him. It was now almost fourteen centuries since Moses
had left the people he had led out of Egypt, after he had showed them the
goal of all their wanderings.

The man stopped at the spot where Moses died and looked ahead of
him, to the West, at the panorama of the Land of Canaan. Almost at his
feet a long thick green line followed the Valley of the Jordan. Further
away, on his right, the fields of Samaria spread across the hillsides and
hid the town of Shechem. Completing the horizon was Mount Gerizim
where the Samaritans had built a temple to their god, who was not the
God of the Jews. In the centre of the landscape was Jerusalem, like a
bottomless pit. There was nothing left but a desolate hill where once the
splendour of Israel had been. Further to the left was Bethlehem, perched
on the mountains of Judaea like a miraculous citadel protecting the Holy
City. Then there was the brownish line of the desert as far as the lights
of Hebron, the oasis where the patriarchs were buried. At the four corners
of the Promised Land were the Roman camps. The land no longer had the
appearance of a place inhabited by a free people.

The man continued his journey northwards. The following day he
reached Pella. The little town reminded him of the treason of a few
Jews who were disciples of Jesus of Nazareth and who in 66, had refused
to take up arms against the Romans—choosing instead to cross the Jordan,
settle there and declare themselves neutral. People were beginning to call
them Christians, but as far as he was concerned they were heretics. They

thought that Jesus was the saving Messiah, but he knew that Jesus was not. Throughout the Roman world the Christians, as the Jews, were regarded with suspicion. The pagans did not like their self-assurance nor their exclusive belief. For some years the Jews and Christians had been persecuted alike by the Romans.

*   *   *

The man knew full well that by fleeing Judaea he was not going into a peaceful world where he would live well. The determination which induced him to go was not self-preservation. It was a feeling of disgust that forced him to leave. He could not bear the sadness of the country nor the artificial optimism of the rabbis.

A few days later he left Palestine territory and began to cross the vast desert-like expanse separating it from Egypt. Unlike Moses, who led the Hebrew people out of the house of bondage, he did not go round in circles in search of the heavenly manna. He joined a caravan of bedouins and went due south until he reached the Red Sea, but did not linger there over the memory of victory that it arouses in the Jewish soul. He finally reached Egypt and arrived at the gates of Alexandria.

Alexandria had more than a million inhabitants; it was crossed by an immense avenue nearly four miles long and some thirty yards wide, and all the streets joined it at right angles. Its five districts were known by the first five letters of the Greek alphabet. A mole over eight miles long joined the quays to the island of Pharos which was dominated by a marble tower, the lighthouse, where a wood fire always burned to show sailors the entrance to the harbour.

The city was the residence of the kings of Egypt, and had been founded in 332 BC by Alexander the Great, rapidly becoming the most famous metropolis of the Greek world. It was the meeting place for intellectuals from all countries—grammarians, philosophers, geographers and poets.

In the museum, a sanctuary dedicated to the goddesses of the arts and sciences, was a mammoth library which held more than five hundred thousand manuscript volumes. Any work coming into Egypt had to be deposited there, and the librarian's duty was to buy systematically all the books he could find. Copiers transcribed them, kept the original text, and gave the owner a copy.

There were fourteen thousand students who flocked to the lectures and lessons given by masters of all the various disciplines. There were exotic plants in a botanical garden, and rare animals in a menagerie. There was an astronomy observatory and an anatomy school where doctors carried out dissection of bodies. There was a gymnasium, a running track and a theatre. This amazing cosmopolitan city was a place where intellectuals thrived, ideas bitterly opposed each other, morals were degraded, where a taste for enjoyment was unleashed, and luxury was encouraged by intense commercial activity.

Jews had been there since the city was founded, either coming from Judaea or from the other areas of Egypt where they had lived for three hundred years. This first nucleus had increased, encouraged by Alexander the Great, who proclaimed that all Jews were full citizens and gave them rights accordingly. Some were prisoners of war who acquired freedom later. Others had emigrated from Judaea during the persecutions of Antiochus Epiphanes. For two hundred years the community constituted an independent body politic recognized by the public authorities and governed by an ethnarch who was assisted by a Sanhedrin of seventy members, in charge of adminstration and justice.

When Rome took control of Egypt, 300,000 Jews, living mainly in the Delta district, still retained all their civil and religious rights. They had many places of worship, and spiritual centres where they were able to practise their religion entirely at liberty. One of the most famous temples was at Leontopolis, not far from Memphis, in a part of Egypt where the number of Jews was especially high. The community had built the house of worship on the ruins of a pagan temple dedicated to a cat-headed goddess. The temple was small, and had the appearance of a tower, and therefore outwardly had nothing in common with the Jerusalem Temple. Inside, however, it was fitted out in exactly the same way. There was the seven-branched candelabrum, the sacrificial altar and the sacred vessels. The offices which were held there involved priests, Levites, prayer, sacrifice and solemn pilgrimages, exactly as at Jerusalem. However, the existence of the temple violated the principle of only one temple for the Jews. The temple at Leontopolis became the religious centre for the Jews in Egypt, but all the same they continued to regard the Temple at Jerusalem as the only religious edifice inhabited by God.

The Jewish population of Alexandria engaged in a wide range of occupations. There were goldsmiths, blacksmiths, engravers, silversmiths, weavers, men engaged in Nile navigation and import and export operations. Jews handled the transit of goods from Africa, Arabia, Somalia and the Indies and exported them in ships to Italy, Greece and the Aegean Sea. The Egyptian wheat which went to feed Rome was quite often shipped in Jewish vessels. Many Jews became soldiers and politicians.

Nevertheless, in spite of a very close human and cultural involvement with the Hellenistic world, the Jews lived out their role as people of the Diaspora. They held in veneration their spiritual and religious home—Jerusalem—recognizing it as their political fatherland. They fulfilled their military obligations in Egypt, but went on pilgrimage to the Temple at Jerusalem. They behaved as loyal citizens, but married among themselves and very rarely gave up the faith of their fathers. In fact, Hellenization was only a superficial phenomenon. The Jews concentrated on utilizing those things from the civilization around them that would enrich their own cultures.

At the same time, the Septuagint or Greek version of the Bible which was undertaken at Alexandria during the second century BC by seventy-two learned Jews, spread monotheistic faith and Messianic hope among the pagans. In contrast to Palestinian Judaism—which was exclusive, tied to the sacred language (Hebrew), and divided from the Graeco-Roman world by a barrier of hostility—stood the Judaism of the outside world, which was open to foreign influences, and freed from the practices, the detailed ceremonies, of the traditional hierarchy. Through their spiritualization of Jewish doctrine, the Alexandrian Jews, with their worldwide vision, transformed a local religion into a missionary religion. They adopted the Greek language and the Greek version of the Bible, which they raised to the dignity of the Hebrew original by maintaining that it was inspired.

East and West were linked together in Alexandria, and the Jews, through their literary and historical works, contributed to the peaceful confrontation of these two worlds which had hitherto not known each other. The Library and the Museum opened up for them a pagan culture, an unknown wisdom. It fell to Philo and the Jewish school of Alexandria to demonstrate that there were numerous affinities between Greek and Hebrew thought, and that Greek wisdom put divine revelation within the grasp of human intelligence.

In spite of this cultural exchange, the Greek masses, turbulent and impressionable as they were, displayed anti-Jewish tendencies. They usually regarded the Jews as foreigners who, since they were gifted with particular skill, had succeeded in obtaining the same rights as themselves. They were jealous of their commercial success and they thought that it was incredible and irritating that they should refuse to merge their faith and the local religion. Monotheism and an aversion for pagan divinities, when confused with atheism, seemed monstrous, and unworthy of an inhabitant of Alexandria.

As a result there were frequent Greek and Jewish disturbances. Under the Ptolemies, in 88 BC, there was a bloody battle between the two communities. Under Roman domination the quarrel took on a doctrinal aspect, since the Jews did not indulge in emperor worship. The fact that they were officially given a dispensation was a scandal. The Greeks, now zealous for Roman religion, attacked the Jews everywhere, and the Jews defended themselves fiercely. The then emperor, Caligula, said that the pagans were right, but he died before he was able to put into operation his plan for making the Jews see reason.

In 66 the entire Greek colony of Alexandria met in an amphitheatre to decide upon sending an embassy to Nero begging him to take exceptional measures in respect of the Jews. To their great surprise, they discovered three Jews who, entirely in good faith, were attending the meeting. They were accused of being spies and were burned alive. Then, throughout the intellectual metropolis of the Empire, angry Jews attacked the Greeks. The fights were often violent. The Prefect Tiberius Alexander, who was a converted Jew and a former Roman procurator in Judaea, sent two Roman legions against the Jews, with five thousand Libyan soldiers who happened to be there. Their orders were to kill the Jews, pillage and set fire to their houses, and in this way fifty thousand were massacred.

This explains why, during the war in Galilee and the battle of Jerusalem, when the fatherland was being swept by fire and bloodshed, the Jews of Alexandria, in spite of rebellious feelings, did nothing to attempt to prevent the destruction of the Temple. They remained quiet, terrorized by the memory of the repression imposed by Tiberius Alexander.

Three years after the burning of the Temple, in 73, armed revolt spread across Egypt. The heads of the community, obeying at one and the same time Rome and the rich Jews who cared little for subversion, had no hesitation in organizing a hunt for the *sicarii*. More than six hundred of them were found and handed over to the authorities to be put to death by Roman executioners.

But in the course of the two years after the fall of Jerusalem, a few Zealot groups who had escaped the massacres in Judaea took refuge in Alexandria. Their strength lay in their reputation as unbeatable fighters, and they kept up the will to fight and be free among the Jewish population.

Their presence and their indulgence in propaganda made the ruling Jewish class cautious, for their interests were threatened by the spirit of rebellion.

Rebels took over Cyrenia during the Jewish revolt which broke out almost fifty years later throughout the Roman Empire and was favoured by the fact that Emperor Trajan was on his way to the Persian Gulf. They put the Roman garrisons in Egypt to flight and then pressed on, not bothering to attack Alexandria, which was not the object of their revolt. The beaten Roman soldiers then took refuge in Alexandria, and their wrath naturally turned towards the Jewish community, despite the fact that they had not taken part in the rebellion. Penned up in a special district, their goods were pillaged and the main synagogue demolished. After centuries of grandeur, Alexandrian Judaism was doomed to economic and spiritual decline. The world of the Mediterranean saw the eclipse of a splendid Jewish metropolis that a rabbi once described as the sister of Jerusalem.

The man finally settled down in this foreign city on which the Jews had nevertheless made their mark. He realized that he was entering a new world where hostility was the rule. But now, in the Diaspora, the Jews were no longer masters of their own fate. Their very religion, in which many saw a chance of survival, was threatened, criticized and forced into silence. Moreover a great theological dispute was about to begin as to whether the Jews or the Christians would impose their faith on the most powerful empire in the world.

As he set himself up in the Delta district, the man felt that he no longer belonged to a nation, but only to a people whose Temple in Jerusalem had been destroyed exactly a century before, and who were now dispersed throughout the Roman world.

*   *   *

In accepting the delay of their dream of spiritual emancipation, the Jews at the end of the second century contrasted strangely with the first Christians who told any who cared to listen that liberation was near, that the Kingdom of God was coming and that the salvation of all those who believed in Him was at hand.

Numerically the Jews no longer represented a powerful body in the Roman Empire. Before the great catastrophe one man in ten under the authority of Rome was a Jew, and there were more than six million of them in the Empire. Until the Bar Kochba revolt there were still five million Jews, but now there were no more than two-and-a-half million. This decrease was the more potent in its effect because of the wide dispersion which had taken place. Previously the Jews had been concentrated in the countries bordering Judaea, but now there were many in Africa and in Europe. In Italy they settled in Rome, Ostia, Genoa, Milan, Ferrara, Bologna, Ravenna, Brescia, Naples, Pompeii, Salerno and Tarentum. They settled in Sicily, in Sardinia, in Spain—particularly in Cordoba and Toledo—and in the Balearic Islands. In France they settled in Narbonne, Marseilles, Arles, Avignon, Uzès, Bordeaux, Clermont-Ferrand, Mâcon, Chalon-sur-Saône, Dijon, Bourges, Poitiers, Nantes, Orléans, Paris and Metz. In Germany they settled particularly in Cologne, Bonn and Ratis-bon (Regensburg). They settled in Great Britain, and on the banks of the Adriatic, particularly in Dalmatia; in Thrace, in Macedonia, in the Greek cities of Delphi, Athens, Piraeus, Patras, Argos, and Sparta; and in Crete.

In Africa, Jewish communities were formed throughout Egypt, in Ethiopia, in Libya, in Cyrenaica, in Numidia and in Mauretania. In Asia Minor Jews lived in Rhodes, Cyprus, Smyrna, Phrygia, Galatia, Syria—particularly at Aleppo—Antioch, Seleucia, Palmyra, Damascus, at Tripoli and Tyre in Armenia. Beyond the limits of the Roman Empire there were Jews in many towns east of the Euphrates, particularly in Babylonia, Assyria, Media and Arabia.

Antoninus the Pious, who succeeded Hadrian in 138, was unable to believe that a people that was numerically so small and so dispersed throughout the Empire or beyond it might constitute any sort of threat to the security of Rome. He therefore decided to rescind the measures taken against the Jews by his predecessor. He re-established the freedom of the Jews to worship and the right to circumcize, though this remained forbidden for non-Jews so as to prevent conversions to Judaism. But the new emperor did not mean to stop at these measures.

Rabbi Simon ben Gamaliel, who was a descendant of the great Gamaliel, led the life of an outlaw, in common with the majority of the scholars of Judaism. He was thrown into prison by Hadrian's men, but escaped and for several years lived clandestinely. Eventually Roman anger cooled. The few intellectuals who had been able to save their lives and their freedom took heart. They issued a manifesto which renewed the appeal that Johanan ben Zakkai made to the people: 'Let anyone who has studied come and teach, and let anyone who has not studied come and learn.' Simon no longer saw why he should live as a recluse. He came out of his hiding place and rejoined his friends and disciples. In common with Johanan, he thought that peace was indispensable if Israel was to settle on a definite corpus of belief suitable for surviving in the face of dispersal and persecution. Thus he decided to collaborate with the Roman administration so as to ensure the necessary conditions for study.

Then the emperor made an astounding decision. He named Simon Patriarch of Israel. It was made quite clear to Antoninus that a Roman emperor should, after so many years of struggles and suffering, realize the pernicious nature of any sort of Jewish authority, whether that authority be spiritual or political. But Antoninus was looking to the future. He was thinking about the Jews of the Diaspora, who, deprived of even the semblance of life in Palestine, would lose no time in finding new revolutionary themes. Moreover the Jews in the East (east of the Euphrates) had always been obedient to an exilarch, a prince of the captivity who maintained that he was a direct descendant of King David. Rome had not succeeded in imposing its authority in the East. If the Jews within the Empire did not have favourable rule from Rome, they would take their orders from the enemies of the descendants of Augustus. Moreover it would be easier to levy the various taxes if the Jews were organized and were held jointly responsible for the collection.

Simon ben Gamaliel was astonished when he heard that Rome recognized him as Patriarch of Israel, a vestigial symbol of the sovereignty of Israel. The patriarchate became the supreme dignity of Imperial Judaism. The Patriarch was in effect an important state official.

Simon soon adjusted himself to the new position bestowed on him. A Sanhedrin was gradually reconstituted, meeting at Oucha. With the agreement of this assembly Simon hoped that he would gradually be able to build a new organization of Judaism. But he had to come to terms with a major phenomenon since the fall of Bar Kochba. The Jews were dispersed, they were more numerous outside the Holy Land than in it, and Judaism now had several centres, even if the memory of Jerusalem was still alive in the hearts of all.

In agreement with the Sanhedrin, the patriarch fixed the dates of the main religious feasts, particularly the Passover, which both the Jews and the Christians looked forward to. He was also appointed to negotiate with Rome the level of taxes and the means of raising them. Politically and administratively the patriarch was an ally of the Romans. Simon ben Gamaliel knew this perfectly well, but he thought that the simple reality of a Jewish authority in Palestine represented for the Diaspora a demonstration of the cohesion and unity of the Jewish people. Moreover the institution seemed to him to be indispensable from an intellectual point of view. The existence of the Diaspora was a reality that would last. It was useless to hope that in the decades to come there would be a movement for the Jews to return to their homeland. The central factors governing this were still as strong as ever. Simon feared that the vast oral tradition formed by generations of learned men as they studied the Torah would be lost if contact was not maintained between the teachers living in Palestine and the Jews dispersed throughout the Roman Empire.

As for the Jews of Babylon, they had no fear of intellectual suffocation. For six centurnes they had studied and their teachers had given authentic lessons. But in the East, too, the Jews were getting further away from the centre of Babylon. There was a general need for a written canon of Jewish knowledge to give precise definition to the customs, manners, uses and religious practices, which constituted Jewish society.

Simon considered that the patriarch must therefore not only see that peace was kept with Rome, but that he should also be the real intellectual master and legislator of Judaism. It was not surprising, in these circumstances, that some monarchical privileges should be extended to both the western patriarch and the eastern exilarch. The differences of course were still enormous. The patriarch was subject to common law and might be judged by the Sanhedrin, but royal honours were extended to him. In places of prayer the scroll of the Law was carried to his seat, whereas all the other Jews had to go to it with fear and respect. The Diaspora liked the idea that a Jewish authority should exist somewhere and that it should be accorded honours which recalled the glory of time past and national independence.

Before he died, Simon invested all his powers in his son Judah. Like his father, he was a learned man. Under his inspiration transcription of the *Mishnah*, the oral wisdom of the Jews, made considerable progress. He took pains to ensure that the analyses reproduced by the learned men avoided the appearance of hard dogma. He thought that a variety of points of view—accounts of discussions, the hesitations of the teacher and the varieties of past teaching—ought to be reflected in the book of Jewish wisdom. Every detail of Jewish life and practice was prescribed, but the instability of human conduct had to be taken into consideration. Every point of Jewish belief was settled, but the scepticism of human nature or the contradiction in man's conduct was taken into account and dealt with.

For the Jews of the Diaspora, as well as those of Palestine, Judaism constituted a unique doctrine and a unique fund of knowledge, but everyone could make his own particular contribution. This absence of dogma induced a definitive intellectualization of Jewish life. In this way the people of the Diaspora symbolically reintegrated the centre of Judaism. Even the Gentiles were frequently interested in these Jewish discussions. Obviously in such cases it was not a question of extending Jewish knowledge, but a love of argument that led the Jews to frequent non-Jews, so as to test the worth of their ideas. Discussion with Jews was held—by the Roman dynasty of the Antonines, as with previous emperors—to be a royal pastime, and the Roman dynasty of the Antonines were no exception.

Gradually the Jews assimilated themselves into the Empire. The question of co-existence between the followers of Moses and the worshippers of the gods of stone had long since been settled. The Jews were not compelled to take part in the imperial cult and did not have to swear before idolatrous emblems when they joined the Roman army. Many Jews were already Roman citizens. Emperor Caracalla, at the beginning of the third century, decided that all inhabitants of the Empire would have the dignity of citizens. Judaeo-Roman symbiosis was once more in operation, thanks to Roman goodwill and Jewish wisdom under the authority of their patriarch.

But the patriarch was not happy. Judah was well aware of the leap forward taken by Jewish learning in recent years, but he was not happy that the Jews of the Diaspora should think that the years of independence had returned. When, in his teaching, he commented on the Biblical sentence, 'The voice is Jacob's, but the hands are the hands of Esau' (*Genesis*, XXVII 22), he said that the voice of Jacob (symbolizing Israel) cried against the hands of Esau (symbolizing Rome).

Furthermore the patriarch was aware of the young rabbis who opposed him, and who one day dared to teach in front of him: 'The Messiah will not come until the two families, that of the Exilarch of Babylon and the Patriarch of Palestine, have disappeared in Israel.'

Before Judah died he invested his son with the rank of patriarch, but did not make him president of the assembly of doctors, since he thought his son's knowledge insufficient. Therefore the doctoral class became more powerful.

The people of the Diaspora saw the difficulties of the heads of the

institutions of Judaism as of secondary importance to the great battle
that was soon to be fought. The Christians were savagely persecuted by
Rome and were beginning to separate themselves from the Jews. They
seemed to be in a good position to attract the great mass of the pagans to
their doctrine of salvation.

*   *   *

As he left his colleagues in the academy, the rabbi—a Pharisee—was
filled with doubt as to the value of setting down in writing the whole of
the oral tradition of Israel. The memory of the Jewish nation was anchored
in the Jewish conscience. The rabbis of the Mishnah had unanimously
agreed not to deal, other than by allusion, with this particularly dangerous
theme as long as Rome was all-powerful. Priority was evidently given to
the commentary on the Law. The learned men of Israel excelled in this
field. They felt perfectly at ease and did not risk reproach for subversive
activity.

But there was the fear lest the religion itself should be attacked by
other faiths which would be able to move with the times. Also, others
might come and proclaim themselves more universal than Israel.

The rabbi thought about the people who believed in Jesus of Nazareth. He had been born three hundred years ago in a grotto in Bethlehem,
on the night of December 25—when the Jews were celebrating Judas Maccabaeus' victory over the Syrians. The victory consecrated a new dedi-
cation of Solomon's Temple, and was traditionally the motive for a feast,
the Feast of Lights. Jesus was, for his first disciples, the Light of the
World. For three centuries the new faith was only known by the Romans
as an appendage of Judaism, which in fact it was. Far from fighting among
each other, the faithful of the two religions had daily contacts. Both Jesus
and his first disciples were Jews, but in the years following his death,
many who accepted his message were pagans, living in the Roman Empire.
After their conversion to Christianity, they often discovered the Jewish
roots of their faith. They were Christians with Jewish leanings, fasting
during the Jewish feasts, observing the Sabbath, and avoiding consump-
tion of unclean meats.

There was also a large mass of pagans living on the fringe of the
Jewish population who had not been touched by the Gospel, and whose
interest was focused on Judaism. These former idol worshippers adopted
the belief in the one, invisible God, attended the synagogues, observed the

Sabbath, but were not converted. They were neither circumcised, nor took up the burden of the Torah.

The religious situation was therefore fluid, and a succession of emperors did not make any distinction between the Jews and the many sectarians around them. But gradually the Christians won their independence from the Jews. The Jews were still in a state of shock after the great defeat and the failure of successive revolts. They exercised a certain amount of reserve in their proselytizing activities. The Christians, on the other hand, who had not indulged in any national struggle, countered Roman paganism with increasing aggression but without ever resorting to violence. Consequently they were an easy prey of Roman cruelty. Their courage in the face of death, their unemotional acceptance of the most horrible torture, impressed the Roman people but left their rulers unmoved. The hatred which the latter reserved for the Jews was transferred to the Christians who had not—in Roman eyes—had the courage to fight, and who could not claim that their religion was rooted in nobility or recognized antiquity. The Christians were newcomers, a *gens tertium* or third class of people. They were persecuted even more than the Jews, since there was no fear of violent reactions on their part.

But what concerned the rabbi of the Mishnah was that the Christians, not satisfied with preaching to the pagans, began to try to convert the Jews. The new converts to Christianity forgot the Jewish roots of their faith. The Christians' main theme was that God had abandoned Israel and that they were the new Israel, sons of the new covenant. The philosophy of Christianity was that the Temple had been destroyed, and the Jews for the most part exterminated. Those who survived were dispersed throughout the world, where they were victims of persecution. The Romans were the instruments of God. The Jews would suffer to the end of time because God had abandoned them. Others had been called to the Divine choice. Those were the people who have recognized in Jesus the saviour of humanity. The Jews had not followed Jesus; and furthermore, although he was born into their nation, in their land, they had put him to death.

The rabbi knew that all the Christians said about the Jews in their talks was false. God had made a definite covenant with Israel, sealed with those very sufferings they had endured in His name and for the respect of His Law. The fact that Jerusalem and its Temple had been destroyed and the nation scattered, proved that Israel had been chosen through trial and tribulation. Israel would always be Israel as long as they continued to say that God is One. As for God's Messiah, he would announce the end of time and the real reign of the Lord. Since the birth of Jesus of Nazareth nothing had even begun to prove that the world had taken a step forward to its salvation. Finally, it was not the Jews who put to death the man who, in common with Rabbi Hillel, preached charity and love of one's neighbour. It was the Romans who had accused him of being the King of the Jews and put him to death by crucifixion—a Roman method of execution.

The rabbis of the Mishnah devoted themselves entirely to the immense task of formalizing Jewish doctrine and practice, rather than contradicting Christian belief. It seemed for the moment the right thing to do. Living conditions for the Jews in the Empire had improved, and the Christian attacks did not harm Judaeo-Roman relations.

But dealings with the Christians deteriorated. In 300, a council at Elvira in Spain communicated to the Christians the order to break off friendly relations with the Jews.

In the year 312, on October 28, the Battle of the Milvian Bridge was fought, thus ending the civil war between two candidates for the Empire, Constantine and Maxentius. Constantine emerged victorious. A few years later, in 321, the Jews had every reason to be thankful for the outcome of that battle, as indeed they had had for the outcome of the Battle of Actium. For under Constantine, the oppression eased.

But in 323 Constantine decided to adopt the Christian religion, not only for himself but for the whole Empire. Rome had now taken for herself the religion of those who, a few years earlier, she had thrown to the wild beasts before delighted crowds. When the Jews heard this extraordinary news they understood how wise the Christians had been never to make war on Rome. At the height of Christian persecution Origen, in reply to those who asked him why Christ had not appeared sooner, would answer that before the Messiah came the world had to be united under the banner of Augustus, the first emperor. The Jews had never compromised on this principle.

Constantine was fully aware of the consequences of his conversion and the imposition of Christianity as the state religion. He forbade the conversion of Christians to Judaism. The renunciation of Christianity was treated as a crime punishable with confiscation of one's possessions. Any attempt by the Jews to take reprisals against another Jew who embraced Christianity was punishable by death.

In this situation the rabbis of the academy calmly continued to produce the Mishnah, the second Law. Far from making it easier to embrace Judaism, they reiterated the problems, taking into full account the new living conditions of the Jewish people in the Diaspora.

If at this time a man wanted to be converted he was asked the following questions: 'What has decided you to be converted?' 'Do you not know that today Israel is suffering, that she is kicked, beaten, persecuted and afflicted with a thousand punishments?'

If he replied in the affirmative—'Yes, I know, and although I am not worthy, I want to share in Israel's lot.'—he was admitted at once. Then he was instructed in some of the easy commandments and in some of the harder ones, and he was told of the punishments for breaking these commandments. They said to him 'Until now you might eat the fat of animals, which is forbidden, without incurring eradication, you might violate the Sabbath without being liable to be stoned. Now you will be submitted to these punishments.' But though he was warned about the punishments for breaking the commandments he was also told of the rewards for fulfilling them. They said to him: 'Know that the world which is to come is not only for the just. Today Israel cannot have too much good, nor have too severe a punishment.'

Constantine took the title of *Pontifex Maximus*, or Chief Priest, and he did not have much trouble in bringing about the gradual disappearance of Jewish proselytizing in the face of Christian dynamism and the facilities for conversion afforded by Rome.

The orientalization of the Empire was becoming more pronounced, and it was with amazement that the Jews learned that Byzantium was the new capital. Once again, they felt deeply the loss of their homeland, and how serious the absence of temporal support was for them. They believed in the universal worth of their religion, but every year on the 9th day of the month of Ab, they wept for the fall of the Temple in Jerusalem.

The scholars who produced the Mishnah were cautious about the advent of the Messiah and his character. This was not only because the revolutionary implication of the idea of Messianic expectation was dangerous for the Jews' safety, but also because the character of the Messiah was hard to determine without a risk of serious error. In any case, the Jews did not ask themselves what God's envoy would be like. As far as written and oral tradition was concerned, the Messiah was of course a man. A few Christians, for their part, also thought that Jesus was a human being and could not be compared with God Himself. The Arians defended this point of view hotly. But the majority of the growing hierachy of the Church did not think this way. The Jews took part in a debate which split the Christians about the nature of God and Jesus. A council met at Nicaea in 325 and came to the conclusion that the Father and the Son were consubstantial—that is, of the same substance. Jesus was God. God was Jesus. The Arians were driven out of the Church.

The Jewish scholars greeted this Christian decision with incomprehension and irony. But some wise men, more concerned with history than theology, were unhappy. Until then the accusation made by Jesus' disciples against the Jews concerned a man, sent from God, but a man all the same. The Jews had rejected Jesus, they had not recognized the man chosen by God to take His last message to men, His new covenant. Thus, if God and Jesus were consubstantial, to reject Jesus or, what was worse, to condemn him to death, was tantamount to rejecting or condemning God Himself. The Jews were no longer accused of rebelling against Christian teaching, but rather they were accused of deicide.

A great deal had happened to the Jewish people since that day twenty-five years previously, when a Roman soldier, in response to an unconscious impulse, had set the Temple which the Jews had built to seal the relationship of God to His people and His earth ablaze. Had the Jews disappeared from history on the 9th day of the month Ab in the year 70? Crushed by Roman might, deprived of their Temple, dispersed and persecuted, had they disappeared as a people for ever?

Epilogue

Gideon Levi is an ordinary soldier in the army of Israel. He settled in the country ten years ago, when he finished his studies at the Sorbonne. His family had settled in France generations ago, but he left them to go to Israel. He was not going as a religious pilgrim, for as far as he was concerned religious practice and belief were non-existent. Nor was he an ardent Zionist.

On Wednesday June 14, 1967, Gideon Levi was sitting by the western wall of the Temple with a sub-machine gun on his lap. This vestige of the outer wall of Herod's Temple remains intact after nineteen centuries. Fourteen huge layers of stone are visible, but there are eleven more buried under the debris of the past glory of Judaea. The wall was increased in height by five recent layers which the Muslims added when they built the El Aqsa mosque. The silvered dome of that mosque winks at the sun, while at the centre of the Temple site itself is the gilded dome of the Mosque of Omar.

The lieutenant in command of Gideon Levi's unit had posted men right across the esplanade. It was going to be a hard day because that morning the Jews were celebrating the Festival of Shavuot in memory of the day Moses gave the Torah to the Jewish people. On that day the Israeli general staff's present to the people who escaped German persecution was simply the right to go and pray at the foot of the wall. Until this moment, the Jews in Jerusalem had not been allowed into the old city. Resistance had stopped, but the Israeli government wanted the invasion of the faithful to be orderly, and to avoid upsetting the Arabs. That was why Gideon's friends, having fought to regain possession of the city, were on guard on the Temple Mount.

The order to take down the last barriers had not been given. Gideon looked at the city that he had never seen in its entirety. White sheets and shirts hung from the windows of the houses. There were a few Arabs in the alleys which Jesus once trod, bent under the weight of the Roman cross. Gideon thought that the Arabs had marked the city with their presence and their religion. A process of orientalization and the decline of the Roman Empire had allowed people from the Arabian peninsula to settle on the remains of the Jewish state. But the Israel that was re-created some twenty years ago would never again allow anyone to rule over this land. That was why it was necessary to fight the Six Days' War, without joy but in faith, without hatred, but with the certainy of being right. During that epic week, every time Gideon saw Arabs defeated or columns of Palestinian women and children fleeing the fighting, he was sad. In his collective unconscious he had already lived the same scenes, but he put himself in the place of a frightened and astonished Arab child. Gideon—in common with all Israelis—promised to be friendly and generous to the Arabs, and hoped a lasting peace would be quickly negotiated.

It was very hot on the Temple pinnacle. Men on guard duty from the previous evening began to relax their attention. Some lay on the ground and tried to sleep in the meagre shadow of the Mosque of Omar. Ascher ben Abraham, who was in command of the men, was twenty-two years old. Pushed back under his helmet he had the traditional curls of the Hasidim of Antwerp. When his parents emigrated to Israel, they quite naturally settled in Mea Shearim, the religious district of a hundred doors, each one opening on a classroom. Since then the study of the Torah had taken on for him a meaning it could never have had in a *yeshiva* or Talmudic school of the Diaspora. It became a genuine reason for living. But when Israel's existence was threatened by her angry neighbours, he obeyed his seventy-five year old master and, exactly like his friends, joined his unit, cleaned his gun and filled his magazine as the yeshiva masters dug trenches on the Sabbath.

Ascher ben Abraham woke his men and called them to him, except for the sentries. But Gideon Levi was near enough to hear the lieutenant's words.

'Our Torah forbids wasting time,' he said, and a groan of weariness was the reaction. Some protested that the war was over, others simply lay down again. But Ascher ben Abraham was not discouraged. 'You are lying down on the holy esplanade where God wanted His Temple built. Let me at least tell you what conditions must first be fulfilled before Israel can rebuild the Temple.' The soldiers looked at each other, mumbling that he must have gone mad from the heat. Some said that they now had to build the country on firm foundations, and not the Temple.

Lieutenant Ascher took off his helmet, put on a skull-cap and began to speak. They all listened.

'Israel has a duty to rebuild the Temple, which is not only the symbol of national independence but also the pledge of the presence of the Holy One, blessed be He, in the midst of His people. But the conditions to be fulfilled are strict. First of all we have to be sure that there are no corpses buried under the esplanade. Now across the generations the people who occupied Jerusalem, sometimes deliberately, have buried dead on this spot. On the other hand, during the battle for the Temple, thousands of Jewish fighters disappeared under the debris. In the first place we must therefore find a way of purifying the place.

'As far as the architectural construction is concerned there is no problem. We have the exact measurements, down to an inch or so, of each part of the building. Unfortunately we are unable to fix the exact site of the Holy of Holies. As long as we are unable to do so, we will not be able to do anything about it. Whatever we do could be a great sin in the sight of the Eternal. Each one of our steps could take us into the Holy of Holies. The Jews ought to be forbidden to enter the mosques of Omar and El Aqsa so as not to risk such sacrilege. Obviously one must also assume that these two buildings, which are sacred for the Muslims, will be moved somewhere else.'

The soldiers burst out laughing, and Gideon Levi first, for no one could even imagine depriving the Muslims of their holy places.

'We must also revive the priestly class, the only ones who may offer sacrifice in the name of the whole of Israel. The Sanhedrin's genealogical tables were lost a long time ago. The people called Cohen today are not all worthy of priestly functions. They have entered into forbidden marriages and have not observed the whole of the Torah.'

'And what about sacrifices?' shouted Gideon. 'Do you intend to start them up again?'

'One would have to study the question very carefully. We would have to find a way of offering to God the material proof of absolute submission to His will.'

A radio message interrupted the lieutenant. In ten minutes the faithful would be allowed to enter the old city. The soldiers got ready to go back to their posts, but Ascher ben Abraham still had this to say:

'In any case, no one can make the decision to rebuild the Temple.

If there were still a Sanhedrin and a family of High Priests recognized as such, if a descendant of David were proclaimed King of Israel—even then no one could undertake to rebuild it. Our tradition says that as long as the Diaspora exists—in spite of the establishment of Israel—only the Messiah will be able to lead the people into the House of God.'

At first it was only a far off noise punctuated by the short cries of the *shofar*, the ram's horn. Then, from out of the maze of tiny streets, a crowd of men in large fur hats appeared, wearing white prayer shawls embroidered in blue, and carrying the scrolls of the Law. They were escorted by armed young men dressed in khaki, tanned by the desert sun. Lastly, at the rear of this human wave forced into a procession by the narrowness of the streets, came men and women in white and coloured blouses, wearing skull-caps or hats. At the centre of this tight mass of faithful was the Chaplain General of the Israeli army, reciting the psalms of rejoicing.

Gideon Levi saw these men coming on like a wave flowing from the depths of his memory. Instinctively he got up and put down his sub-machine gun. The noise had reached a climax. Everyone was praying for himself and for all Israel. There was a silence, lasting only a moment. Then the Jews ran to the Temple, to the spring from which they came. Those who got there first clung tearfully to the vestiges of the House of the Eternal, the others reached out to touch the holy stone with the tips of their fingers. Further back the Jews organized themselves. Groups formed around rabbis and answered 'Amen' to a hallowing for the dead of Israel. 'May His name be great and holy.'

The non-religious in their many coloured clothes wept and prayed too. They went from group to group and embraced each other. One thought inspired all the Jews. For the first time in almost nineteen hundred years the people of Israel, organized as a state responsible for its own destiny, extended its sovereignty over the Temple of Jerusalem. It was not the prayer of various individuals that went up to heaven, but that of a people descended from the kings and prophets of Israel, whose thanksgiving was no longer merely a concession from a controlling authority. Israel and its prayer were free.